Salesian School Song

All Hail Salesian School to thee
By time endeared the more
Our hearts shall ever loyal be
To thee and friends of yore
And memories that shall never fade
Wherever we may roam
Shall rivet fast the friendships made
In youth and boyhoods home
Long live O Alma Mater
On thee may blessings rain
And may thy sons hereafter
And may thy sons hereafter
Bring honour to thy Name

SALESIAN SCHOOL, BLAISDON HALL, LONGHOPE, GLOS.

Anthony Brady - 2016

Anthony Brady

Blaisdon Made Me

Book 2 of the series
"Scenes From An Examined Life"

© 2017 Anthony J. M. Brady
Cover: Petra Schubert
Editing: Petra Schubert

Publisher: tredition, Hamburg, Germany

ISBN
978-3-7323-9647-4 (Paperback)
978-3-7323-9648-1 (Hardcover)
978-3-7323-9649-8 (eBook)

Table of contents

About the Author

Anthony J. M. Brady was born in 1940 in London. He retired in 1994, having completed a career in local government as a Principal Officer Team Leader with the London Borough of Camden, from whose Chief Executive's Department he had been seconded to the Department of Health & Social Security (Resettlement Centres) for 15 years. In 1997, he moved to Northern Ireland and lives in Brockagh, Tempo, Co. Fermanagh.

A Communitarian, he participates in part-time voluntary work involving social reconstruction, advocacy, renewal and reconciliation. His first writing in print was an essay in the London Chest Hospital Staff Magazine: Shakespeare and Medicine (1964). His first letter to a newspaper appeared in the Catholic Herald and this led to a series of polemical exchanges in its letter's page about the American/Vietnam War with the writer John Braine (1969/70). His first writing fee was for a book review: Caring on Skid Row by Anton Wallich-Clifford – the founder of The Simon Community, commissioned by The Catholic Herald (1974).

Subsequently, (1981-1986) he had letters published in The Catholic Universe, Hackney Gazette, The Guardian, The East Ender, The East London Mercury and The Greenwich Mercury on topics such as Apartheid; Drug Addiction; Homelessness and social justice issues. Many of his letters on topical issues have appeared in The Fermanagh Herald and The Impartial Reporter.

The Guardian printed four of his letters (1987-1990). One highlighted the threatened closure of a service for adolescent mentally ill people at The Maudsley Hospital; another two were arguments against reduction of hospital provision in London and the fourth objected to the euthanizing of the first person in England to have feeding methods legally withdrawn to assist his death.

A Paper entitled helping the Resettled Person with a Relapsing Drinking Problem was published by the Charity, Good Practices in Mental Health. ISBN 0 948445297

Tony began to send out creative work for the first time in 2003. A short story: 'Sister of Mercy' was published by the weekly magazine "Ireland's Own" and in 2004 an historical profile about Angela Burdett-Coutts: Queen of the Poor, was published by the bi-monthly magazine "Ireland's Eye". Both publications are popular in Ireland and the United States. Since 2003, he has had published (in anthology) numerous poems in various publications under the aegis of Forward Press: Anchor Books, Triumph House and New Poetry.

Dogma Publications have also published his poetry in anthology. Other works comprise "Castle Coole - Millennium Evocations - A house tour in verse", "Thank You! Miss Hutchinson - Collected poems", "Cast Out Remorse!" - Short Stories, Essays and Commentaries.

Acknowledgements

While writing this book, I received great encouragement from former inmates of *Saint Joseph's Home, Enfield*. They have read drafts of my work and made comments in an Epilogue, serving to validate through their own experience, these recollections that recall my years 1945-1952.

Though dealing less with personalities than I, the late *Norman Taylor* has described faithfully and accurately the prevailing social conditions revealed in historical data through his researches in the archives held by The Crusade of Rescue's successor organization, The Catholic Children's Society. Norman has also revealed much concerning the scarcely documented life of girls in other Homes who were the separated siblings of boys at St. Joseph's.

Peter Landsborough compiled the St. Joseph's Home, Enfield, **Glossary of Slang**. It contains over a hundred expressions: he began this during the 1960's using his abilities for writing and flair for correspondence with former Enfield boys scattered around the world; he has also met many former Enfield boys through his yearly attendance at the Salesian Old Boy's Association Re-Unions at Blaisdon.

Mike O'Brien RIP 2017 - a published poet – has written numerous letters to me recalling his Enfield experiences and commented on my own. A series of searing published poems – Intimations - illuminate his early life in St. Joseph's Home and his transition to a Gloucestershire farming experience. In keeping with his contemporaries and later generations of boys – who share an unbreakable line of friendship developed over half a century – Mike has described in a poem this bond as inspired by *"The long years of harshness, the sudden change from grief gave common cause that bound us with as strength beyond belief"* **(The Brotherhood)**.

Michael McKenna has been encouragement itself. His letters, comments and opinions on drafts I have sent him, have been enormously moving.

Norman, Peter, Mike and Michael, these my memories are the sum of your parts. In the words of the Blaisdon School song: *"Rivet fast the friendships made in youth at boyhood's home..."*

I thank particularly *Sammy Hayes* who was an Enfield and Blaisdon contemporary. I am indebted to *Carol Roper* of The Catholic Children's Society, who inherited the records of The Crusade of Rescue, for her assistance and acquainting me with other source material to aid my researches.

Sister Joan – Archivist – The Daughters of Charity, Mill Hill, London, graciously provided the St. Joseph's Home and associated photographs.

The regular contact with *Fr. Sean Murray SDB, Charles Springett and Terry O'Neill* through their work for **The Blaisdon Old Boy's Association** has been inspirational.

For their technical help, I thank the staff of the public libraries in counties Fermanagh and Tyrone: *Mairead McKenna, Amanda Hamilton, Doreen Dunwoody, Fivemiletown, Gerry McKenna, Lisnaskea and Ken Newman, Mobile Library Services.* A special Thank You to *John Cloughley*.

Finally, none of the books in this series would have been produced without the dedication of *Petra Schubert* as my editor.

Synopsis

T he "*Scenes from an Examined Life.*" is an autobiographical series. In 1939, a child is conceived out of wedlock in Northern
Ireland. The protestant father is married with 10 children. To
avoid scandal the catholic woman moves to London. She is forced to
abandon her six-month-old child in a London Cathedral. The Crusade of Rescue, a Catholic benevolent society, arranges fostering
and in the years 1945-1952, the child is cared for in St. Vincent's
Home, Feltham and St. Joseph's Home, Enfield, Middlesex, run by
the Daughters of Charity of St. Vincent de Paul.

The mother was disfigured by fire in a childhood accident. The
Orphanage Sisters discourage mother and child contact saying she
frightens him. He is told that his mother has died in an air raid and
his father in the war. He is led to believe that his mother's accident
was a penance, and that when he is older, he will be disciplined by
men in expiation for her sin. The boy exists in an often harsh, con-
fusing and unforgiving environment, subjected to many humiliating
examinations of personal effects and frequent "examinations of con-
science". He experiences various forms of abuse, is bullied and often
lives in fear. Even so, he makes fun of things with his companions
and makes lifetime friends.

Though the mother cannot see her child, she lives in the house of
a Jewish couple as a nanny until their 3 children grow up: two become doctors and the third a pharmacist. She stays on with the couple until they retire. Meanwhile, the child is moved when 12 years
old (1952) to a residential vocational training school in Blaisdon,
Gloucestershire, which is run by men: The Salesian Fathers of Don
Bosco.

The boy is treated kindly by the priests and lay brothers and his
progress in school leads the Rector to propose moving him to one of
the Salesian colleges. He opts to leave when 15 and is given a job on
the school farm as a stockman. The farm manager, Fr. Dan Lucey
becomes a surrogate father to him: when 17, he learns of his origins
and experiences a spiritual crisis. Fr. Dan encourages him to visit
Lourdes "to take his mind off himself". The experience there and

subsequent four pilgrimages motivate the young man to resolve to dedicate his life to others.

On the last one, he works with a Belgian Jesuit Père Raoul Lievens, who becomes a spiritual mentor. Against the advice of Fr. Dan, he leaves the farm where he has worked from 1955-1961 and goes to live in Belgium. From working in a TB sanatorium at Mont-sur-Meuse, Ardennes, he is accepted as a student in The Institute of Tropical Medicine, Antwerp and qualifies to work in the former Belgian Congo.

Books of the series "Scenes From An Examined Life":

Book 1 *"Of What is Past"*

Book 2 *"Blaisdon Made Me"*

Book 3 *"Near And Dear To Someone"*

Book 4 *"Nothing Matches - But It's Home"*

Chapter 01 – Blaisdon Hall-Arrival

B laisdon made me, Blaisdon shaped me,
All that she had, she gave me again.

"Daddy, I want you to talk about when you were a boy."

"Yes. How far back do you want me go?"

"To when you were twelve years old. Tell me a mouth story!"

It was at times like this, when his son was lucid and reflective, that the father experienced a special closeness to his child that transcended all the confusion and pre-occupations that usually possessed his son's attention. His son had specified a "mouth story" as opposed to a story that was read to him from a book. As the father related his own boyhood memories, the distractions that usually held his son in thrall, dissolved away as he became rapt in concentration on every word as his father drew him into a world that engrossed the child.

"This story begins one day in 1952 when I was twelve years old and I was told by one of the nuns that I was leaving St. Joseph's, and moving to Blaisdon, in Gloucestershire. The person who told me this was a nun. Do you know what nuns are?"

"Yes. They are sisters who looked after you when you were a boy."

"Why was that?"

"Because you lived in an orphanage."

"Yes. The nun said that the time had come for me to leave the orphanage, which was in Enfield, Middlesex and that from now on I would be cared for by men. They would be priests and brothers and they would be very hard on me because I needed discipline. I was afraid and asked the Sister if I was going away on my own? She said that I would be going with another five boys and that everything was arranged and that I would leave tomorrow."

The next day, after pinning our names and the destination Gloucester to our jackets, the six of us: John Loftus, Peter Noone, James Meenagham, Ronald Daly, Donald Bibi and me, were put in a taxi and one of the nuns came with us to Paddington Station. Several times, during the journey through the London streets from Enfield in Middlesex, the nun leaned over and said to us all: "Yes, it's discipline you need and Jesus, Mary and Joseph the Salesians will give it to you!"

"When we got to Paddington Station a porter led us to a train standing at the platform and we got into a carriage. From a large bag, the nun gave us a packet, which she said were sandwiches for the journey adding that if she had given to them to us in the taxi we would have eaten then by now. She said that we must not get off the train – even though it would stop at Swindon and Reading - until we got to Gloucester where, we would be met by a man, all dressed in black. The Sister stayed on the platform and through the open window said, 'as we are early and the train does not leave for 15 minutes, we will say one decket of the Rosary from the Joyful Mysteries' She held the beads in her hands and then a whistle blew and her last words to us were: 'Discipline, yes.. Discipline, that's what you need and Jesus, Mary and Joseph that's what you will get. Liberty Hall is over, Blaisdon Hall... discipline... God Bless you!"

"Was it a steam train or a diesel train that you went on?" said the child.

"I recall the smoke and the hissing steam noise and the clicking sound of the train wheels passing over the tracks," said the father, 'but what I remember now was how quickly we opened our sandwiches and ate them. In fact, we had eaten them long before we got to the first stop, which was Reading. Later we stopped at Swindon then finally we got to Gloucester.'

"Was the man in the black clothes waiting for you?"

"When the train came to a stop we waited in the carriage until a man in black clothes came to the window and said: 'I am Brother Edward Barron and I am going to take you to Blaisdon'. Presently, we got onto another train and Brother Barron said that the journey would be about ten miles. He pointed out Gloucester Cathedral as we passed it and the River Severn which we crossed by a bridge at a place called Over. Soon we came to a station called Grange Court; later on I will tell you another story of how I rode the last working pony - at the farm on which 1 was to work - to that very station where is was weighed. However, it is a long and a sad story. We set off again passing through open country and as the train slowed, Brother Barron drew us to the carriage window and pointed out Blaisdon Hall in the distance.

It was a prominent house set high on a slope in a great park with many trees before it. Behind it was a forest of tall fir trees that framed what was a mansion with a high tower. 'That cannot be a school' I said 'It looks like a palace'. 'No: it is a school' said Brother Baron as the train came to a stop at the station called Blaisdon Halt. 'We will walk from here' he said, as the train steamed away. From a distance, we could hear the sound of a bell. 'That's the school bell which is on top of the school tower and it's ringing the Angelus' said Brother Barron."

"What's the Angelus, Daddy?"

"It's a prayer that is said at six o'clock in the morning, at noon, and at six o'clock in the evening".

"Brother Barron stopped walking. He made a sign of the cross by touching his forehead with the tips of his right hand then his left and right shoulder and finishing with both hands joined on his chest. He prayed out loud saying: 'Angelus Dei nuntiavit, qui concepit de Spiritu Sancti... Ave Mari gratia plena...' I was used to the nuns leading the Angelus and saying the prayers with them but this was the first time that I had heard it prayed in Latin. By the time Brother Baron ended his prayers the bell had stopped ringing and he said that we would all have a turn at pulling the rope that hung from the tower to the ground floor of the school entrance hall. "Let us walk on up to the school".

"I have never forgotten that walk. Every hedge was a wild extravagance of leafy growth thronged with birds. Behind hedges, fences and walls were cottages and houses. Their facades were like faces: the doors mouths and the windows eyes. Paths, some crooked, some straight, led up to each from different sorts of gate. Brother Barron named some of the houses: The Forge, The Old Mill, The Tann House. I stared at each one as we filed along each side of the road that had no pavements.

Sometimes we came to gateways from where we could see long fields that stretched as far as we could see. We rested and looked over gates into orchards that were in blossom. It was magical: thrilling sensations fixed forever the immediate experience of sights and sounds in the memory of an enchanted twelve years old boy, who had suddenly been plunged into the country from the fastness of a city existence".

"Did you see any animals?" asked the listening child.

"I remember we passed a huge barn with a low curved metal roof. The smell from it was strange yet warm and pungent. There was a sound of movement inside. We stopped to look through thick wooden bars that faced the road. Standing on a floor of straw, I saw a group of large cattle with curly hair: as they breathed, steam seemed to come out of their noses. One of them had a huge head, ran at the bars and butted them. I was scared. 'That is a bull and the other beasts are bullocks' said Brother Edward, 'they belong to the school farm which is run by Father Dan. You will be able to see the whole farm after lunch. The school owns hundreds of acres of farmland with woodlands. That's the village public-house and Gideon Price - the landlord.'

The sight of Gideon was startling. He stood looking over a door, which was cut in half under a sign saying *The Red Hart*, which swayed in the breeze above him. He was ten times more frightening than the bull. His eyes were black and bright. His hair was white and thick and his chest was covered with a beard that was square and reached his trousers belt. In his mouth, I could see a long white clay pipe and from his nose was pouring not steam but thick smoke. Suddenly he spat, stepped back and in an instant, what was half a door became a whole one which remained slightly open and through its gap, a small terrier dog stood watching us.

By this time, we had walked through the village of Blaisdon and on turning a corner, saw a strange looking house, which was built in the shape of an arch through which the road ran straight into a parkland. Brother Barron said: "That's the Lodge." As we walked through the arch, he pointed out the ornate metal gates, which were held open, and just then a tractor roared up and as it passed us, the driver called out "Howdy folks!" 'That's Brother Joe Carter. You will meet him later and Father Dan also because after lunch you can go and see the farm'.

We walked up a long winding drive. Soon, to our right on higher ground, we saw a church, with a clock face. The bell in its tower struck the half hour. The drive curved to the left, as we passed under the largest conker trees we had ever seen, and straightening, led to the castle-like Blaisdon Hall which came ever nearer as we walked along. To our left was a vast park with groups of massive trees. Away, into what seemed an endless distance, the sun glinted on a winding river. 'There is Westbury village' said Brother Edward, and beyond it is the River Severn'.

As we paused to take in the distant vista, we became aware of a group of boys coming to meet us. As they came close, we recognised them and ran to meet them. They were boys we had known at Enfield. We all expressed trepidation at what awaited us. It increased when "Bulldog is waiting to meet you" said one of our former chums. "He's alright", said another. "Father Wilson is his real name." Soon Brother Barron was introducing us to a priest with thick paw like hands and a purple face. "Welcome to Blaisdon Hall! You are just in time for tea!" He shook our hands and led us to the refectory where we were introduced to all the boys. We ate our meanwhile Father Wilson read in a loud booming voice some pages from an adventure book: Biggles Sweeps The Desert.

When the meal was finished, Father Wilson said that Freddy Cove, an ex-Enfield boy, would take us to our dormitory and show us around the school, the grounds and the farm.

"Is that the end of the story Daddy?"

"No, son. It is the beginning."

Chapter 02 –Blaisdon Village

Blaisdon lies about 8 miles South West of Gloucester on the edge of the Severn flood plain. Before the Norman Invasion, it was known as Blethes Dene, meaning 'wooded place'. The village turns towards the rich farmland of the Vale of Gloucester, and its land is predominantly fertile, once with many orchards growing the "Blaisdon Red Plum". Always small, the village is protected by the barriers of the River Severn and the Forest of Dean. The centuries were hardly noticed here, and even the Civil War of 1642 passed it by.

Stud Farm 1956-View To Blaisdon Village Church, Plum Orchard, r. Pig Field I

The early houses were timber framed, built with Forest Oak, but a disastrous fire on 7th July 1699 destroyed most of the village. Subsequent rebuilding was in stone or brick, but some timber-framed buildings remain. In the 18th Century, the village estate was owned by Robert Hayle and John Wade, whose daughter Anna Gordon ran the estate until its sale in 1865.

The Great Western Railway connected the village to the Hereford-Gloucester branch line in 1852, and steam trains could be heard in the village until 1964.

A rising industrialist, Henry Crawshay, acquired most of Blaisdon in the 1860's, and rebuilt the nave of the church in 1866. Blaisdon Hall was built in 1876 for his son Edwin. It is situated on an elevated site overlooking the village. By 1890, the Hall and most of the estate had passed to Peter Stubbs, who built the entrance Lodge to Blaisdon Hall, the Village Hall and the Forge.

At the Stud Farm, he bred *Blaisdon Conqueror* - the world's largest *Shire horse*, whose bones lie in the British Museum.

On his death in 1906, Peter Stubbs' eldest daughter, Mary Helen McIvor, inherited the Main Hall, and built the estate houses in the village centre and the Gamekeeper's Lodge. With her husband Colin, she ran the Estate until her death in 1928.

Salesian School of Agriculture and Trades Blaisdon Hall. Glos.

The Salesians of Don Bosco acquired Blaisdon Hall as a seminary and boy's agricultural and horticulture school in the 1930's, and ran the Stud Farm as a dairy and arable enterprise.

A valued part of the village community, all visitors were made welcome at their home, until they left in 1995. Hartbury Agricultural College took the Hall until 1999 when it returned to private ownership.

Chapter 03 –Saint John Bosco

Giovanni Bosco (Don Bosco) {1815-88}: founder of the Salesi-an Order of Priests and lay-Brothers. Born in Piedmont, Southern Italy, he was the youngest son of a peasant farmer who died when John was two years old. He was brought up by his mother in extreme poverty. When he entered the seminary in 1831, his clothes and shoes were provided by charity. He was ordained priest in 1841 and soon settled into his life's work: the education and apostolate of boys and young men, especially of the working class.

Turin was the principal place of his activity. Persuaded by the rector of a seminary in Turin - *Joseph Cafasso* - later canonised a saint - to abandon his dream of foreign missionary work, he was intro-duced by him to both wealthy benefactors and to the slums and prisons, which would gain most from his ministry. *John Bosco* was appointed a chaplain of a Refuge for girls. He devoted himself also to the needs of young men especially on Sundays. His attractive, charismatic personality soon drew many to his Oratory and his evening classes.

Soon he resigned his post as chaplain and lived in poverty with his mother and about forty destitute boys in the Valdocco area: later he opened workshops for training shoemakers and tailors. By 1856, their number had grown to 150 resident boys with four workshops: there were also 500 children attached to the Oratories and ten priests to teach them. An eloquent preacher and a popular writer of great skill and diligence, John Bosco also had a reputation as a vi-sionary, a wonder worker and one with an extraordinary gift for handling difficult youths without punishment but with a gentle but effective firmness.

Don Bosco often used to take boys on Sunday expeditions in the country, with Mass to start with, followed by breakfast and open-air games, a picnic, catechism class and Vespers to conclude. He be-lieved in the value, especially for deprived urban boys, both of con-tact with natural beauty and the uplifting power of music. In 1850, he began to organise a Congregation, which was formally approved in 1874; at the founder's death fourteen years later it numbered 768 in sixty-four houses in both the Old and the New World. Now it numbers many thousands and specialises in pastoral work and schools of all kinds, including technical, agricultural and ecclesiastical seminaries.

As a church builder, Don Bosco achieved the apparently impossible by heroic trust in Providence to provide the necessary finance. One of his triumphs in this regard is the church of *Sacro Cuore*: completed shortly before his death. Another achievement was the foundation of an Order for nuns to do work for girls similar to that achieved for boys by his own Institute. It was called *The Daughters of Our Lady Help of Christians*, spreading to most of the countries, where the Salesian Fathers were at work.

In 1888, the funeral of Giovanni Bosco was attended by a large proportion of the citizens of Turin. 40.000 people visited his body as it lay in state. He was canonized in 1934. His Feast Day is 31st January.

Source: The Oxford Book of Saints

References: G. B. Lemoyne & E. Ceria, Memorie biografiche di Giovanni Bosco (19 Vols., 1898 -1939; Eng.tr., 1964-   ); E. Ceria (ed.), Epistolario (1955-   ); Lives by A. Auffray (1929, Eng.tr. 1930, H. L. Hughes (1934), Henri Ghéon (1935, Eng.tr. 1935), and L. C. Sheppard (1957). See also articles in N.C.E and Bibli. SS.

Chapter 04 –The Blaisdon Prefecture

ather Harold Wrangham. (1906-1991) – Rector. Formerly Prefect of Studies at Salesian College Battersea, London. A tall, saintly austere man. As he prayed in the chapel, his balding head in profile reminded me of a bust of the head of a Roman emperor. The back of his cassock was always shiny due to his many hours of working in his study.

After saying morning Mass he would, weather depending, walk up and down on the terrace outside the chapel and through its bay windows, boys could see him saying his Rosary or reading his Breviary - The Holy Office. Sometimes, he walked in conversation with *Lady Crawley-Boevy*, Blaisdon School benefactor and catholic wife of protestant *Sir Lancelot* of nearby Flaxley Abbey. *Father Wrangham* was looked upon with awe and reverence by all the boys and was paid the highest respect by his Salesian community of priests and lay brothers. He only participated in football and cricket on official Feast-Days. Playing as a halfback, cutting in sharply from either side, he usually got himself out at cricket when he knocked off fifty runs: mainly boundaries. He wore his old school (Farnborough Salesian College) cap on such occasions. He often played tennis on the lawn leading to the long passage of trees known as The Monk's Walk. A snuff taker. He met with every boy in his office at least once a year. See "Going to Father Rector."

Father William Wilson. (1915-1963) - Prefect of the House. Nicknamed "Bulldog." His main role was Bursar and he was responsible for the functioning of all the school's domestic arrangements. He had two offices. One was for administration where the telephone switchboard was and another where the strong room/safe was situated. Operating from the latter place he reluctantly provided the boys with special items such as new boots, blazers etc. These sessions were conducted after tea on Tuesday evenings where, assisted by a hovering Brother Edward Barron, Bulldog employed an approach, which was essentially a battle of wits. "Boots!" he would roar. "Boots!" "Yes Father, worn out Father." "Take them to Brother Gerald and get them soled"! You had to make a strong well-argued case to get any clothing or footwear replacement from him. "I need a pair of new socks Father". "Socks! Socks!" Yes, Father, they've got spuds in them. "Darn them boy, darn them!" He was tall and heavily built, with huge beefy hands, and his face was usually purple in colour yet, belying his nickname and intimidating presence, he was essentially a gentle giant and was only helping boys to be assertive.

When on Refectory Supervisor duty Fr. Wilson read aloud during the earlier part of the meals. He particularly liked the Biggles books by W.E. Johns and adventure stories featuring Bulldog (loud cheers) Drummond. He loved nothing more than helping George Austin, grounds man and landscape gardener, mow the lawns with the Dennis petrol mower or leading groups of boys on coppicing work in the extensive woods surrounding Blaisdon Hall. A supporter of lowly Derby County FC and when playing cricket sported the cap of Derbyshire County Cricket Club. Bulldog had the most unusual bowling action. Basically, it was a "throw".

To liven up House-Matches the House Master would sometimes put himself in to bat or take over the bowling. This was a signal for all to retire to the boundaries. On one such occasion, Kevin Giblin umpire at the bowler's end called "No Ball" six times consecutively. Each time Fr. Wilson responded "Discipline Mark - Giblin!" When batting Bulldog informed the umpire that LBW did not apply in his case. At football, he was judged "a bonker": toe punting the ball in whatever direction he happened to be facing at the time. He was the Alban House Master when I was its Captain and a very enthusiastic motivator for its success in all areas. He was always handing out marks.

Once in the refectory he called out "Discipline Mark, Brady". "What was that for Father?" I enquired. "For golloping!" he replied. I was eating my food too fast! When Father Wilson was saying Mass, he would stop in mid-action, stare round, and glare at the noise-maker. Instead of achieving the desired effect his face prompted a fit of uncontrollable merriment in the watching boys. He liked to cycle. One day, one of the boys fixed the rear wheel of his bike so that when Bulldog started peddling it went backwards.

Father James Docherty. (1910-1999) – Prefect of Religion. A Scotsman who as a boy worked as an apprentice rivetter in the Clyde Shipyard. He was responsible for all the boy's religious training aspects and an absolute stickler for correct altar and chapel behaviour. He arranged all the Mass Server's Rotas and posted these on the school notice board every Saturday morning. A boy had only to shout out: "I'm/you're on the "bucket" - the knick-name for the incense senser/ the thurible - for him to go into a temper and spray bad marks everywhere. He would stand at the back of the chapel and intervene directly in a ceremony such as Mass or Benediction if a boy serving at the altar was sloppy or inattentive or showing irreverence.

We were taught religious doctrine in class by him via The Catechism and he presented every new boy the Salesian Prayerbook. The most intense demonstration of his piety was when in chapel he intoned the Prayers for a Happy Death on the first Friday of the month. This one, number four from a total of thirteen invocations is readily recalled: "When my face, pale and livid, shall inspire the bystanders with compassion and awe, and my hair bathed in the sweat of death, and stiffening on my head, shall forbode my approaching end, Merciful Jesus - have mercy on me.

Fr. Dochery taught appreciation of religious art and introduced us to the main heresies that the Catholic Church contended with during the centuries. He would often refer to "Fenelon & Bosuett...." It was not unusual for him to be reading religious works that ranged from the heavy Summa Theologica by St. Thomas Aquinas to lighter fare such as Morris West's in the Shoes of the Fishermen. I remember him particularly as a brilliant inside forward and a supporter of both Celtic and Rangers football teams.

Father John Connolly. (1920-1991) - Prefect of Studies. Conducting the school brass band and producing plays and pantomimes was when he was happiest and entirely approachable. Outside these times he was, as Headmaster, responsible for discipline and liaised daily with the four Housemasters of Alban, A'Becket, Fisher and More. Although rugby was never played the school was run like a quasi-Public School. Lines were handed out: I shall not talk after The Goodnight -100 times. Prep. Cross Country Runs; House Matches; Sports Day, Army Cadets, Choir, Founder's Day, Refectory Duties; Country Walks, Chapel, Infirmary; Matron.

Our Headmaster's personal approach for maintaining systematic order was a most incisive sarcasm. He oversaw the system of good or bad House conduct, merit and discipline Marks that were dispensed by priests and lay brothers and entered on a sheet displayed in each classroom. These were totted up every Saturday morning and the ritual of Marks took place when he toured the classrooms handing out finely honed, humiliating sarcasm to recalcitrant and motivational encouragement to good achievers.

The winning House was awarded High Tea or discounted Tuck-Shop. Those with five or more bad conduct Marks got - as a last resort - good old-fashioned public school corporal punishment in the bend-over position. This was dispensed by Father Connolly in his office witnessed by a priest who noted the number of bamboo cane strokes in a Punishment Book. The strokes were delivered on trouser protected buttocks: usually no more than two - "Six of the Best!" was extremely rare. I can remember one such Saturday when I was caned but the second occasion was particularly memorable.

One Friday in Lent, the lunchtime boiled fish was most unusually foul and led to a shameful event after the meal. Outside the boys refectory was a hatch that served the Community refectory: it was always closed when the boys exited en masse. Someone in the dense melee banged on the hatch and when it was opened by Mr. Higgins ("Wiggins" because of his toupee) and instead of compliments, he got a lump of fish full in his face. The repercussions were most serious. Father Connolly cancelled all that afternoon's activities and demanded the culprit admit his action or be named by his fellows. Nobody complied. General detention was declared and a 24-hour ultimatum issued: Confess or Inform. Otherwise, the whole school will be caned!

The deadline passed and every boy lined up for the bend-over and two strokes of the cane: one for not owning up another for not telling. I was 25 in the line of 45 and thinking Father Connolly would be off guard I put a copy of the Beano inside the back of my trousers. Alas, with the first stroke I was "sounded" and ended up getting a total of four: two delayed until the following Saturday. Later, there was a collective apology to Mr. Higgins who stressed his strong regret about the caning while forgiving whoever was responsible for, what everyone agreed, was insulting and extremely regrettable behaviour.

I remember all four priests with an affection and admiration that endures. Their influence has enhanced my life. Father Rector, because he was holy and kind, gave me my first job. Father Wilson taught me how to be assertive without being aggressive. He stimulated my appreciation of the plays of William Shakespeare when he directed the school production of Julius Caesar. Father Docherty passed on his deep love of the Catholic faith and inspired the beginnings of my appreciation of Christian Art. Father Connolly shaped my personality and moulded my character in ways that made it possible for me to exercise authority with responsibility and a balanced sense of justice in my professional life. He was an extraordinary caring person as I learned later when I was working on Stud Farm. He moved from the position of Prefect of Studies to Infirmarian and looked after me whenever I was ill.

I cannot forget that these men dedicated their lives to the care and education of boys and remained faithful in their vocation. I was fortunate and privileged to have been placed in a situation where I came under their influence. Their example and the words they spoke from the Epistle when celebrating their Mass on the feast day of their founder St. John Bosco are a continual reminder and blessing:

"Whatsoever things are true, modest, just, holy, lovely, of good fame, if there be any virtue, in any praise of discipline, think on these things. The things which you have both learned, received, heard and seen in me, These do Ye, and the God of peace shall be with you" - *Lesson of St. Paul to the Philippians. iv, 4-9*

Chapter 05 – Every Good Boy Deserves Favour!

All the priests in Blaisdon were, in their various ways, substitute fathers to a boy such as myself, who had never known a real identifiable father in the familial context of a loving family. *Father Daniel Lucey* was my special surrogate father. I took to him on first sight the first day I was in Blaisdon. After lunch on that day, the boys in my arrival group were taken down to the farm. Earlier, we had been shown a half life-size white marble statue of Saint: *Don Bosco*, which stood in a niche in the front hall below a portrait of *Don Micheal Rua*, his successor. However, a much more sympathetic representation of the saint was to be found in the chapel: a gold framed oil painting, above the altar, which was dedicated to him.

Our guide, *Freddy Cove*, led us across the fields towards Stud Farm and Harvey's Acre - the sports and playing field. Soon we were close to a man pacing lengths and placing spikes among deep lush grass. He stopped and waited for us. We were introduced to - not a workman as we had supposed - but the priest in charge of the farm. His hand put forward in greeting was big and hardened with callouses. His face was brown, his eyes had a blue twinkle and his hair was grey. His whole demeanour radiated kindness. I thought immediately not of the statue in the hall but his likeness to the portrait we had seen earlier in the chapel. As he placed his hand on my shoulder after learning my name, I said to him *"You are Don Bosco!"* He laughed and replied: *"Don Bosco is a saint - I am a simple priest to be sure and all!"* The attraction was instant and from that meeting I was to remain permanently under the spell of this man who was known to all as Father Dan.

He then played his first joke on me. The purpose of what he had been erecting before stopping to speak to us now became clear; he got us to help him. We were each given a spike and followed him as he paced out a measured distance. On each metal spike topped with a white porcelain pigtail head there was a foot-piece to aid its insertion in the ground. We pressed on these and soon a line of spikes ran across the field. Fr. Dan then threaded a fine wire through the whole of the line and connected it to a battery. He lined us up, placing me last in the line with us all linked hand in hand. Taking the hand of the boy closest to the fence, he then touched the wire and everyone laughed when I shouted out and recoiled as an electric shock was transmitted to me.

I was electrified too by *Father Francis Rodgers*: Musician, footballer, teacher and friend when I eventually left school. He was an all-round enthusiast. From Lancashire, he was a great fan of The Hallé orchestra conducted then by *Sir John Barbirolli* - "Barbersbrolly". "Cursing Flagstone" for *Kirsten Flagstad* the opera diva, was another boy's howler. Sir Thomas Beecham was often mentioned. There are many anecdotes about him. In rehearsal, he once said to a woman cellist: "God has given you the most beautiful of instruments between your legs and all you do is sit there and scratch it!" Fr. Rodgers told us that one. Years later, I learned its double meaning. Sir Malcolm Sargent was also admired.

Fr. Rodgers often praised his predecessor *Father Grace* for setting a great tradition of performing music and its appreciation at Blaisdon Hall. He told us much about the lives of the great composers' warts and all. The sacred and the profane were considered and weighed in the balance of his objectivity. The mistresses, the artistic back-stabbing, the interpretive betrayals and the composer's idiosyncrasies were redeemed – in his opinion - by the divinely inspired genius that created musical masterpieces. His particular tour de force in class was to act out a Prelude by Rachmaninov. The music describes a man who is buried and awakes in his coffin. He would put the disc on the gramophone - the one with the winder, an inserted needle and large horn and play the part of the hopelessly trapped buried alive person. This always led to a lively diversion about Transylvania, Dracula and catalepsy. All extremely memorable for its excitement. His music lessons were a highlight of the day.

Our music teacher, animated with his subject, would enter the classroom and with a flourish chalk A.M.D.G. on the corner of the blackboard. Of course, we all knew the Latin: Ad Majorem Dei Gloriam - To God Be the greater Glory. AMDG? "All Music Derives from God!" he would say. He linked ideas to strings of letters to aid the memory. All boys taught by him will remember the acronym for music notation: EGBDF - Every Good Boy Deserves Favour and GDAEBF - Great Dogs and Eagles Bite Fiercely.

Fr. Rodgers was an accomplished violinist. He introduced us to Paganini, Paderewski, and Fritz Kreisler. Yehudi Menuhin, from whom he had taken lessons, was particularly admired. He liked Les and Mary Paul who were making completely new music with the electric guitar. Pablo Casals was a favourite also. Chopin in his works for the piano was unequalled. In his view, the top contemporary orchestral conductor was Arturo Toscanini whose protégé Guido Cantelli was the coming man. His musical taste as communicated to us was catholic in its range and appreciation. He would play us discs of Mantovani, Louis Armstrong, Ted Heath, Geraldo and Joe Loss. He loved black American music and the crossover success from the opera Carmen to the popular musical Carmen Jones. George Gershwin's Rhapsody in Blue was another favourite. Russ Conway, Winifred Atwell and Semprini at the piano were played to demonstrate style and interpretation. And so on.

The brass band and its musical tradition was a genre through which he traced back his musical roots to a boyhood in Manchester. He played all the band instruments with equal facility holding a particular preference for the cornet and English horn. I vividly recall unforgettable times when the band played on the Hall garden terrace or on the lawns under the great red copper beech. Fr. Rodgers would be wearing a white handkerchief knotted at its four corners to keep the midges off what he called his Bobby Charlton wisp: he was a dedicated Manchester City fan. In his view, Harry James was the world's best trumpet player - Eddie Calvert despite his very popular 1950s rendering of Roses are Smiling in Picardie - a pale imitator.

As Choirmaster, Fr. Rodgers distilled through its voices and dedicated practice the transcendental beauty of sung masses and thrilling devotional plainchant that echo in my memory to this day. For the visit of the Rector Major - Don Ziggiotti - in 1954, he composed and set to music an Italian hymn of welcome: O Pietosa. Some of the words I wrote down in a diary I kept at the time: Cara Madre del signora Madre sei del nostro bene. Tu bene vene in quanto pene vive afflitto questo cor. He also arranged the music for the pantomime songs and the concerts known as Academies; these were regular showpieces for the variety of musical talents presented by priests, lay brothers and boys.

None of the boys of that time will forget the friendly rivalry with his walking companion *Father Pat McGrath*. As Housemaster of Fisher Fr. Rodgers, vied with "Mc Ginty's" Becket. The two of them were always among the boys in the playground playing football with a tennis ball. They both had a trick of trapping the ball up their cassocks and carrying it rapidly toward to score from close in against the goal painted on the wall of the school porch.

On the football field, Fr. Rodgers was a masterly player. A brilliant floater of the ball to wherever he wished to place it and able to head it to any spot. He was an encouraging referee always commenting positively on a boy's competence and ability. He played lawn tennis equally well as being a fine cricketer. Model. Mentor. Motivator.

As Dormitory Master, he had his room adjacent on the first floor level of the tower where he kept his sewing equipment. It was not at all unusual to see him darning socks and stitching boy's clothes. Once, when the School Bursar Father Wilson, nicknamed "Bulldog" refused me a new pair of trousers he took my torn pair at bedtime. By morning, he had sewed a full seat patch on them and left the garment ready to wear when I woke up. Wheedling a pair of new boots out of Fr. Wilson required a miracle and he would put in a word to his other particular chum, Brother Gerald Clifton, the school cobbler. Master and Servant...

I was lucky in having my ex-music teacher as a friend when I left school to work at Stud Farm. Being there, I was able to continue in regular contact with him. He would often come down to the farm for a walk usually with *Mc Ginty* or *Brother Gerald* and comment on the progress of the pigs. I would make them a cup of tea in the farmhouse. As I didn't smoke or drink I could afford to buy records and he became my first music appreciation mentor. He advised me to buy music that moved me and not to intellectualize: leave that to the critics, he would say. I looked forward to *Father Rodgers* being a friend for life. But long it could not be. Early in 1958, aged 47, he was diagnosed with an incurable kidney disease. He told me that he had less than a year to live. There was no curative treatment.

There were great consolations in the support of his community, his faith and his music. I longed to help him and be of service. I lent him on permanent loan my EKHO record player and my records. That September I was able to give him one momentous gift: concert tickets for The Hallé Orchestra in Gloucester Cathedral conducted by Sir Adrian Boult. Brother Gerald came too. We went in Ronnie O'Connor's Lanchester car; he dropped us off and picked us up after the concert.

It was a magnificent setting with near perfect acoustics. *Mike Turnbull*, a Blaisdon Hall past pupil, was organist and played as the huge audience settled. The repertory comprised Tintagel - a tone poem by *Sir Arnold Bax*. Nimrod - The Enigma Variations by Edward Elgar. Symphony No.4 "Italian" Second Movement - *andante con motto* - Brahms. "Fingal's Cave" Mendelssohn. Symphony No.8 in B minor "Unfinished" First Movement – *allegro moderato.* Schubert. Finally, The Pastoral Symphony by Beethoven. Always the optimist Father Rodgers emphasized in his post-performance critique the music's soaring divine themes and together we shared and revelled in them. But when alone I was tormented by the music's profound brooding heart-breaking undertones resonating with the inevitability of death.

Father Rodgers died on Christmas Eve. I was feeding the pigs and through a December fog, heard the slow sad toll of the Hall tower bell. Later, I saw him for the last time in his sick room that looked over the beautiful lawns. He was laid out in sacred vestments on his deathbed. It was the first time that I had ever looked upon the face of a dead person.

Through the love of music, that he opened my mind to, Father Rodgers lives on in that love always. He was buried at Beckford Hall near Worcester, where he had studied as a theologian. My Memento of him is his photograph surrounded with the heads of many of my school chums of that time.

"When words leave off, music begins." - Heinrich Heine

Chapter 06 – Remembrance Of Wars - Armageddon Anticipated

The Commemoration & Remembrance of the Blaisdon villagers who gave their lives in the two Great Wars was held on the nearest Sunday to 11th November. The village War Memorial is situated opposite The Lodge - an impressive gated arched dwelling - forming the main entrance - to the drive, which leads to Blaisdon Hall. Directly facing the War Memorial is a life-size crucifix set in a rising bank. Down this approximately quarter of a mile way, The Salesian School Army Cadet Force and school brass band marched from the Hall entrance for the annual Parade & Remembrance Ceremony.

Shall they return to greeting of great bells

in wild train-loads?

A few, a few, too few for drums and yells

may creep back, silent, to still village wells

up half-known roads.

Protocol gave precedence to the villager's observance at the Memorial and the Church of England Vicar had led their Service of Dedication at the Eleventh Hour. The usual 10.30 am Parish Solemn High Mass was celebrated earlier in the Hall chapel and the cadet squad was ordered to "Fall In!" at 11.00 am sharp on the drive outside the boy's refectory. The cadet force Sergeant, depending on which year, would have been Freddy Cove, Derek Reilling, Sam Hayes or Peter Caine. Uniformed Father William Boyd was local Commanding Officer (delegated) assisted by lay Brothers Charles O'Donnell and Thomas Docherty: both wearing navy blue Civil Defence uniform. We, who owed our lives to The Fallen and Spam – Special Processed Argentine Meat -, were totally reliant on them in the event of the Four Minute Warning, which was to precede an atom, hydrogen or nuclear bomb being dropped on 1950's Gloucestershire.

Father George Hilton in an army Chaplain uniform with 2nd World War decorations officiated. He waited within the front hall. A pre-inspection was completed by Fr. Boyd. The evening before had been passed in assiduous furbishing of belts and gaiters and brassoing of buttons, badges and belt clips. With the brass band and choir grouped under the tower entrance, everything was ready for the arrival of the Honorary Commanding Officer: Colonel Forde - Retired - The Gloucester Regiment.

Soon, in visible distance down the drive a long open staff car driven by a uniformed army chauffeur came into view and drew up at the Hall entrance. The band led by Father Francis Rodgers (Choirmaster) and conducted by Fr. John Connolly (Prefect of Studies) struck up and to the tune of *"Willkommen"*, Fr. Hilton descended the steps, saluted and welcomed Colonel Forde as the honour guard - escorting the colour party of the Union Jack and Papal flag – presented arms with 303 Lee Enfield rifles. His inspection complete, the Colonel then pinned poppies on each cadet and returned to his car where he was joined by Fathers Boyd & Hilton. The military precision of everything was very impressive. Colonel Forde signalled with his baton and the march to the village cenotaph began. At this point the Hall car driven by Bro. Alan Garman - in Civil Defence uniform - containing Father James Docherty (Prefect of Religion) wearing his black tasselled biretta and assisted by 3 boy servers, thurifer and two acolytes, went ahead.

With the Sergeant leading the two-abreast squad and wielding a brass tipped staff the squad wheeled left to pass the staff car. At that precise moment the band struck up Colonel Bogey and the squad at the command, "Eyes Right!" passed Col. Forde who rose and acknowledged the salute. Responding then to the command, "Quick March!" the squad and Band followed by Brothers Charles and Thomas, with the staff car party bringing up the rear, continued down the drive. At a respectable distance all remaining "civilians" i.e., priests, brothers, boys and distinguished visitors followed in procession. When this group got to the bridle path about 500 yards down the drive they peeled off and cut through the park to assemble near the Lodge: Brother Gerald Clifton (Sacristan) carrying the ornate tasselled processional parasol shepherded the choir.

Meanwhile, the cadet force-marched on towards the village. On their left flank, the marchers passed the gentle upward sweep of Cinder Hill: a perfect battlefield in a general's dream. Soon the turning at the lily pond and the great almost leafless sycamores and horse-chestnut trees was reached and in sight of the village-church, the Sergeant called a halt. Four buglers then sounded Reveille. From here, the Lodge was visible and the squad proceeded in slow march to muted drumbeat and came to attention just beyond the arch to allow Col. Forde's party to stop directly under its shelter.

Calling the squad to attention the Sergeant ordered "Present Arms!" and Col. Forde completed another inspection. Fr. Boyd and Fr. Hilton stood to attention each holding a wreath. Fr. Docherty led the prayers and sprinkled holy water assisted by the servers dressed in red cassocks and white cotters. Their candles flared briefly in the breeze, guttered and died. The band played *Abide with Me* as Col. Forde accepted the wreaths from both Chaplains and laid them at chest height on the Memorial alongside those of the villagers.

Through the fresh green laurel leaves, entwined with red poppies that formed the wreaths the names of the remembered villagers stood out:

1914-1918

John Owen Bullock   *Harold & Oliver Jones*

George Hopkins   *Frederick Parslow*

Edgar Dowding

1939-1945

Edward Dowdall   *Ronald Bowkett*   *William McNamara*

James Langrell   *Kenneth Hill*

The last two names are those of Salesian School, Blaisdon Hall, Old Boys.

Sheep gazed inquisitively through the Memorial's ironwork and a ram stared intently at the sheepskin that cushioned the big bass drum slung from the drum major's shoulders. The bullocks pastured in the park had charged alongside the railings in the footsteps of the band prancing and cavorting in great excitement. Now stamping about hidden by a clump of rhododendrons they added their own unique chorus. Even they however, observed the Minute's Silence. Then to the bugle call of The Last Post, they renewed their bellowing contribution rising to a crescendo as the band accompanied the choir in The National Anthem.

The villagers had gathered to observe at this point, where three public lanes converged. The local policeman - his bicycle resting against the post office wall - controlled the rare passing car with black and white sleeve chevrons waving and contrasting somberly with the colourful uniforms. The two small children of George Austin, resident Blaisdon Hall landscape gardener, with his wife Beryl, peeped from the small window over the Lodge Arch.

Then, with a final presenting of arms and general salute, Col. Forde returned to his official vehicle and departed up the lane in the direction of Hinder's Corner accompanied by Fathers Boyd and Hilton. They were destined for The Gloucester Regiment Headquarters and further official duties; Innsworth R.A.F. base and Patchworth military camp respectively. The nearby church bell tolled; the Angelus bell rang out from the tower of Blaisdon Hall and the mournful whistle from a good's train passing under the bridge at Blaisdon Halt echoed through the village.

Presently, Brothers Charles and Thomas took command and "At Ease!" led the procession back to the Hall, where all were stood down, and lunch was taken. In the afternoon, the military atmosphere was maintained as the House Teams: Alban, Fisher, Becket and More played football against each other as The Army v The Navy and The R.A.F. v The Royal Marines on the sloping park pitches. The la crème de la crème of the cadets and band members played at Harvey's manicured flat playing field against a crack team from the priests and brothers or the Oratory, which was formed from young adults living in the villages of Blaisdon, Longhope, Flaxley and Huntley.

While most were unaware, a few boys spotted the Civil Defence members of staff climbing into a tarpaulin-covered lorry and leaving down the back drive; speculation was that they were heading for hush-hush exercises deep in the Forest of Dean or a secret bunker beneath nearby Nottswood Hill.

The day came to a close with a full house of priests, lay-brothers, villagers and boys in the wooden concert hall – a former army hut – where a patriotic film such as "The Charge of the Light Brigade" with Errol Flynn or "In Which We Serve" starring Noel Coward.

I am indebted to Roger Etherington - a lifelong Blaisdon village resident - whose family home was The Forge, for providing me with the names inscribed on the War Memorial. I had contacted him about Blaisdon Remembrance Sunday in which I included a poem by Wilfred Owen, whose words from the final stanza of The Send-Off begin this memoir.

I conclude with a personal effort to sum up in poetry the emotions I feel as my mind goes back to those days in Blaisdon during the 1950s when the villagers - who never returned from the two Great World Wars - were remembered.

Did They *give* Their Lives? Or, Were Their Lives *taken* From Them?

Wars Remembered-Armageddon Anticipated

The boy soldiers formed up in line:
The Sergeant inspected each in turn.
Colonel Forde (retired)
took the salute: the cadet's
drilled colour party moved off.

Towards the village Cenotaph
the troop marched on,
and as the band struck
*up the tune **Blaze Away***
flocks of pigeons rose
exploding into flight
spreading like shrapnel
to enfilade the distant trees.

Crackling gunfire
echoed in the woods
and pheasants beat
from cover plunged
to earth, killed
in fern and bracken
by weekend shooting
party's fusillade.

At the War Memorial wreaths rested
where villager's names inscribed on stone
are listed Unforgotten. The church bell
chimed an end to silent minute. Then a bugle
call died away and birds sang out an anthem.

Tony Brady

Chapter 07 – Going To Father Rector

As schoolboys, each boy had a yearly progress interview with the Rector: it went like this. I ascended the beautiful wooden carved main stairs and was admitted to his study/office and sat across from his great desk.

Fr. Rector: "Ah! Our Anthony! Our Anthony! Hm. Hm. Do you pray to our Lady?" *"Yes, Father Rector."*

Fr. Rector: "Do you pray to St. John Bosco?" *"Yes, Father Rector, every day."*

Obviously pleased he would lick his lips and exclaim: "Capital! Capital! By-Jove!"

I stared at the leather bound books in a glass case behind him. Then: "Ah! Anthony! Do you pray to Mary Help of Christians?" *"Yes, Father Rector. I like serving mass on her altar. My favourite."*

"Capital. By Jove! Capital!"

Father Rector's nose twitched and he smiled. Then he took up a shiny looking box from his desk, opened it and with thumb and finger took up a pinch of fine powder. He tapped his brown stained digits against the inside lid of the box then placing the same fingers to each of his nostrils took a deep sniff.

As the holy priest relished whatever the pleasure it was that he derived from the snuff, I looked out through his study window and could see the great ox-bowe bends of the River Severn miles away. Now Father Rector fixed his eyes on me in a direct stare: they seemed to have become much brighter.

He spoke again: "Our Anthony! Hm. Hm. Our Anthony! Do you say your morning and night prayers?" *"Yes, Father Rector."*

Nodding and joining his hands together as if about to pray he would ask: "What about your ejaculations?" At that time in my life, this could only mean one thing so the answer must have been: *"At least 10 times a day Father."*

There was another term for what Father Rector was seeking as we were often reminded to make our aspirations, which were short acclamations of devotion expressed silently to oneself or whispered to the sacred images of Our Lady or various Saints who we were surrounded by. These ejaculations attracted indulgences, which accumulated and assured a shorter period in Purgatory on the way to Heaven. But when later I recounted the meeting with Father Rector to the older boys, I was puzzled when they creased up with laughter when I got to the ejaculations bit.

Finally, Father Rector would ask: "Do you pray to Saint Dominic Savio?" Having received a satisfactory answer there was just time for another pinch of snuff and it was clear that the interview was over when he said: "God bless you! Pray for me my son. Our Anthony! Our Anthony! Hm. Hm."

When I was fifteen years old, going to Father Rector signified my last meeting with him as a schoolboy, for after completing the usual routine, Father Rector offered me a job on Stud Farm as a "stockman" following recommendations from Father Dan, with whom I had been working during free-periods since I came to Blaisdon in 1952. I jumped at the offer even though Father Rector counselled that I consider continuing my education in a Salesian College: he wondered whether I would prefer to transfer to Battersea Salesian College?* He advised me to think about this and let Father Boyd - Bursar - know my decision. I went straight down to Father Boyd's office but as he was away, I had to sweat on the decision of YES to farming until the following day.

So, I left school and moved down to Stud Farm. I had my own room - for the first time in my life. There was a slight delay; I slept for a week or so in the dormitory upstairs with a couple of wayfarers taken in by Father Dan. One of whom - "Scouser" Harold - helped me paint its walls: he included the metal bed which was just like the one I slept in at Enfield. I had never been as happy as now. I had all that I wanted: a job, money and work that I loved. My ground floor room window looked directly onto Periwell Field and Rookery Wood.

I began work on 25.5.1955 as a pigman. I took over a herd of several hundred head, under Father Dan's supervision, from Paul Studd who had just signed up for National Service: he had succeeded John Boden. Paul was to die young in Malaya where he was serving in the British Army. Within months of leaving, he was killed in a plane crash over the jungle. John Boden was known for his hobby of bird nesting and collection of their eggs. He also kept ferrets in the Dog Loft above the pig meal shed. I went out with him several times on his rabbiting jaunts.

My weekly wages came to £2.18s.2 p. after deductions and my keep. On 28.8.55 they were increased to The National Farmer's Union rate of £3.5s.0p. I worked at Stud Farm until 29th December 1961 when I left Blaisdon to live in Belgium. I wanted for nothing and began saving for a bicycle in a Post Office Account that Fr. Boyd opened for me.

*My eldest son completed his secondary education there. Later, he graduated Master of Arts & B.Ed., from Edinburgh University.

Chapter 08 – Men They Were-To All The Country Dear

I lived and worked with the late *Brother Joe Carter SDB* during the years 1955-1961. He was responsible for all things mechanical that operated at Stud Farm. He was a brilliant mechanical engineer, machine fixer and a driver who could achieve the most amazing feats of skill on an agricultural tractor. At one time silage was drawn from the fields on buck-rakes and deposited in pits alongside what was once known as the largest covered barn in the whole of the West Country.

Bro. Joe's tour de force was to make the tractor stand upright on it back wheels in the pit as he balanced the loaded buck-rake before releasing its trip handle. It was a spectacular and daring operation and if miscalculated the tractor would have toppled backwards and certainly fatally crushed him. The cutter/blower forage harvester made the buck-rake less used and I remember Father Rector saying that it reduced greatly the likelihood of Bro. Joe being killed.

He was at his peak when I knew him even though he was a broken man in terms of health and fitness. He suffered greatly with his back and stomach and despite spells in hospital continued to work all hours. In those days, there were no women to care for us - up to 10 men living in the farmhouse - when sick. When he took to his bed, which was rare, I tended him as best I could, while assisting Father Dan.

Fortunately, Bro. Joe was a great reader. As a break from spiritual reading, he loved the Readers Digest and I used to buy him Time Magazine & Life, which kept him abreast of all things American and international. He fostered my literary interest too and honed my verbal dexterity.

Part of our relationship was the cultivation of a mutual witheringly sarcastic, caustic, vitriolic and vocally inventive - yet good-natured antagonism. As a pigman, I was lowest in the farm's pecking order and the butt of everyone's scorn: the tractor drivers were of the elite. Even so, Bro Joe's endless repartee and wisecracks benefited me greatly in later life as I eventually broke out of a crippling shyness to achieve articulacy and literary competence.

Bro. Joe had a capacity for quoting poetry at length and I read and memorised much in order to keep up with him.

Roger Allen-Dermot Hayden-Billy Udell-Author-Lawrence Stanton-Tim Mahoney- 1957

I was in charge of the pig herd at the Salesian farm attached to Blaisdon Hall: 40 sows, each with its own name, two boars and about 300 followers comprising piglets, weaners, gilts for breeding, porkers and baconers. It was a first class piggery: excellent clean and warm housing with the sows and their litters allowed to free range in the orchard and their own meadow. We always got three A's at Nailsworth from the Pig Marketing Board. I used to go to the slaughterhouse in the haulier's lorry: Marfell's from Ruardean, to

accompany my lovingly nurtured porkers and baconers and ease their parting into the irrevocable process and preparation for the butcher's shops.

Stud Farm was a model of good agricultural practice in its time and the local Young Farmers Club's members used to spend study days there advised by Fr. Dan and Bro Joe.

I worked 7 days a week and on my half day, I would regularly cycle 10 miles to Gloucester City. In those days, there were three cinemas: The Gaumont, Regal and Rialto. Sometimes, I managed to get the three programmes in during an afternoon and evening. A snack in the Cadena Cafe was a regular event with an occasional visit to Berni's Restaurant and for the special occasion Don Pasquale's.

The last train back to Blaisdon Halt from Gloucester Central was at 10-30 pm and you could put your bike on the train. I always used to leave it in the Left Luggage Office while about the city. Sometimes my mates and me would cycle from Blaisdon to Cheltenham and catch a Play or Musical: curtain up at 7.30pm then pedal back afterwards: 40 miles round trip in an evening. I was expected to narrate to both Fr. Dan and Bro. Joe all the screenplays, plots and filmic action.

The farm was a haven for homeless people and Father. Dan and Brother Joe Carter used to give their own clothes and footwear to the destitute. The farmhouse provided shelter, recuperation and work in season to wayfarers. Father Dan is for me ever epitomised as a character, which I paraphrase from the poem thus:

"A Man he was to all the country dear... More skilled to raise the wretched than to rise..."

His house was known to all the vagrant train: He chid their wanderings but relieved their pain. The long remembered beggar was his guest. The broken soldier, kindly bade to stay sat by the fire and talked the night away. Pleased with his guests, the good man learned to glow and quite forgot their vices in their woe; careless their merits or their thoughts to scan His pity gave ere charity began". Oliver Goldsmith - The Deserted Village.

We had no television until latterly and the best entertainment in the long evenings about the farmhouse fire was provided by our guests who told us all about their travels and escapades. There was a chapel attached to the farmhouse and Fr. Dan said Mass every day at 6.30 am. Both he, Bro. Joe and Bro. John Wrigley were up at 5.30.am to perform their spiritual duties: reading and meditation and, in Fr. Dan's case, the first of the 4 hour-long readings of the office of the Breviary. I often served his morning Mass and if Fr. Dan had recently given away his shoes or boots he would be wearing wellingtons under his cassock as he set off to hear 7.30.a.m confessions at the boy's Mass in the Salesian School, Blaisdon Hall.

Most days, I started work on the pigs at 6.30 each morning and in the winter often had to break the ice in the swill bins. The attached poem attempts to recapture the flavour, sensations and atmosphere of the winter season. On Saturday afternoons during the football season, I played centre forward for Longhope in the North Gloucester League. After home games, I cycled back to the farm to feed the pigs. The Teams were composed of mainly farm workers and miners and we played all over the Forest of Dean.

The pitches were often rough fields. The style of play was tough and physical. According to the Gloucester Citizen's football correspondent, I was something of a talented player - and once scored 60 goals in the 1958/9 season: a record. Bro Joe encouraged and supported me. I last saw Bro Joe at his Golden Jubilee celebration in Blaisdon and he had become very frail. He was one of the dozen or so men and women of whom I think lovingly each day. I shall remember him as long as I live. It is a precious privilege to have known him and to have been influenced by him.

The community life did not come easy to him. Indeed, his superiors in my time were often desperately concerned about his health and excessive working hours and used ploys - short of imposing Obedience - to get him to participate in community life. One of the best was putting him in charge of the Tuck Shop where he was able to deeply endear himself to boys in the wider scheme of their development and relax a little in the company of his community. He was certainly one of the most admired lay brothers in his time and an enduring Salesian model and mentor.

Bro. Joe was loved and respected by the Blaisdon villagers and was consulted by a wide range of local farmers and our rural neighbours. By all accounts, the present Blaisdon village is largely a wealthy dormitory compared to the 1950s. So there will be few if any that need the couple of hundredweight of potatoes, link box of manure for necessary garden-grown vegetables or a trailer load of logs that Bro. Joe in his spare time dropped off to those struggling to get by. Even less will remember that in the depths of snow bound early winter mornings he was out and about clearing the roads with a combined scraper and brush, which he had devised and attached to his tractor.

Once in a high rainfall Spring he saved two village cottages from flooding: one was "Ma Lane's" next to the Old Mill House. He and Brother Allen attached a pump - one they had modified themselves from ex-Army wartime kit - to the power take off of a tractor and worked hours through a deluge.

These then are some memories of my life with Bro. Joe on the farm and a time that was ours and is ours no more. So many of those who knew him then are dead: Father Dan Lucey SDB, Bro John Wrigley SDB, Mr & Mrs Pat Tobin, Bill Harte, Paul Studd. In the village: John & Ruth Magee ex SDB theologian & teacher, Bertie Bucket, Albert Pittock, Ted Watkins, Cyril Baggott. There are so many unsung acts of Christian community that Bro. Joe evinced. HEARD MELODIES ARE SWEET BUT THOSE UNHEARD ARE SWEETEST.

Lawrence Stanton-Alan Ferry-Author 1958

Winter Morning

Now Autumn's kiss is Winter's bite,
my lips crack as I breathe
the chill morning air;
on the orchard gate a silken sieve
sways: a spider tugs its lair
on rusted bars, silvered overnight.

Pigstyes sleep: windows double glazed
with frost glint back
the sun's bright gleam
over the tractor's bonnet a sack
has frozen stiff as oaken beam
from its pen the bull roars, morning dazed.

Up the farm drive on urgent call
- diesel fumes hang in the air -
tractor tyre prints in the snow
lead to village church and from there
the road is cleared by Brother Joe
'neath gated Lodge to Blaisdon Hall.

Silence: I mix the pig's herd morning meal,
from a wall warm looking cats stare
hungry at the steaming swill:
the fattest of them gnaws a hare
snared that night. When air was still
and freezing I awoke and heard its dying squeal.

Stud Farm – Blaisdon – Gloucestershire 1957

Tony Brady

Chapter 09 – A Labourer Worthy Of His Hire

Pat Tobin came to Stud Farm as Head Cowman from the Tibberton, Taynton, Newent part of Gloucestershire circa 1951,taking over from John Mc Crossan who had left for Ireland. As far as I know, when Pat came out of the Royal Navy - where he served as a turret gunner - he worked for a farming family name of Bradley. Pat idolised the Bradley's who had treated him well. His wife Joan was a Bradley I believe. They had one child Denny when they came, Patsy and Sylvia followed during the years to 1957. As a family, they lived in the house at Harvey's Farm, which was situated in the centre of the village and a short distance from the Red Hart pub. The house between theirs and The Rectory known as The Dairy was occupied by the parents of Brother Jan and his brother called Stefan. Bro. Jan was a brilliant electrician and electrified the Hall and Stud Farm during the 1950s including some houses in the village.

Pat had a weather-beaten face. His most striking physical feature was his thick jet-black head of hair and hirsute body. He had fine teeth once but privations while on wartime battle watch led to stomach ulcers, which ruined them and often plagued him. Joan was stocky, plain and very down to earth. She was a loving mother and very tolerant of Pat's weakness for the cider. She would go to the pub and get his drink for him. I remember this I often sat in the taproom talking to Elsie -Licensee - and her husband, Frank Hogg, as she would come in for fresh stocks. Joan never drank alcohol herself.

Their home was very rough and basic with no refinements whatever. I remember for a number of years being expected to attend there every Friday night to watch T.V. Pat loved "Take your Pick" with Michael Miles which was followed by "The Army Game" (Bootsy) Alfie Bass, (Snudge) and the Sergeant were particularly appreciated. As guests in their home, we often felt awkward and embarrassed because Pat tended to be coarse with Joan calling her: "the old scrubbing brush". I suppose it was meant in terms of endearment but it was uncomfortable for me then. Pat would be very put out if we - other farm workers and me - did not turn up for what was a standing invitation. Eventually we got our own TV at Stud Farm...

Iris Hogg – Author - Elsie Hogg - Margaret

Joan and Pat's children were lovely and we were very fond of them. Fr. Dan saw to their religious education and they attended Mass in the farm chapel most Sundays at 9.30 in the morning. Joan was not a Catholic then. I heard that Fr. Dan eventually received her "into the one true faith". For a time Pat and Joan were often short of money and Fr. Dan helped them out on the QT. In an inspired move, he engaged Joan as dairy supervisor and this was certainly a solution and great boost to the family finances and Joan's self-esteem. She was excellent in her work always.

Pat too was a person whose standard of work was always excellent. He had a natural affinity for animals and a patient temperament, which brought out the best in them. When he arrived at Stud Farm the dairy herd was mainly mixed crossed Shorthorn and Friesian stock; there were some Ayshires and Herefords too. Pat gradually introduced by Artificial Insemination methods a full bred pedigree Friesian herd, which produced the highest butterfat milk content yield in the whole of Gloucestershire - according to the Milk Marketing Board at the time. The three original standing bulls were sold off and an Aberdeen Angus bull bought in from Perth, Scotland. Fr. Dan and Pat went up there to a sale. This breed produces a small hornless calf and was perfect for first calvings: these were kept on to beef stores age. Second calvings were then by AI. The pedigree calves hand reared by Lawrence Stanton initially, later by Joan, were retained as breeding heifers.

Johnny Dunbar – Vincent Faulkenbridge(Shaw) – Author

By 1961, the Stud farm Friesians were known far and wide as best quality maintained stock. Each cow had its own nameplate above its head in the 40 standings milking byre. Its milk yield was shown and level of feed concentrate required. Pat was particularly skilled with first lactating heifers: these can be awful vicious kickers but he was brilliant in his management of them. The herd was a great achievement and source of pride to everyone on the farm. All due in most part to Pat's assiduous care.

Pat was a highly qualified user of all the farm hand tools. His hedge trimming and laying were legendary. Each Spring he and Johnny Dunbar, his cowman assistant, cut the hedges - both sides of the road - perfectly from Stud Farm, past Bertie Bucket's, through

Stanley all the way along Hinder's Lane to Board's farm. His rick building in hay and straw was of the highest standard not to mention his neat use of the winter silage knife on the pits where he had spread the spring grass out on so thoroughly and smoothly. Pat was an "all-rounder" in every farming skill. He had trained with horses and rarely drove a tractor. Although I never developed an affection for Pat, I always considered him a model fellow worker who I respected totally.

When the herd was dispersed at the sale of the farm in the early 1960's - I was in Belgium then - Pat returned to Bradley's and stock management in the location of his old haunts. Anything I know about him from then on is vague and based on hearsay. I heard that his alcohol dependence went from severe to chronic - it had always been mild to problematic - when Joan died young of cancer. At least she was spared Pat's tragic end: he fell into the path of a passing vehicle and was killed.

I choose to remember the best of Pat Tobin and the wealth of his achievements. Only people like those who knew him can appreciate the importance of farm work done to the best of a person's ability. Pat set himself the highest standards and always sought to maintain them through practice and example. One particular feature of his horticultural outlook, which would go down well today, was his prophetic views about organic vegetables. Fr. Dan let Pat have land next to George Keyse's high brick wall on the Harvey's field side. Here he tended a most productive vegetable garden. This was a sight to behold and we often ate the rewards of Pat's good husbandry, which he brought to our farmhouse table.

Pat Tobin served and fought for his country and suffered poor health as a result of terrible conditions he experienced on the seas off Russia. We who were spared such experience admired him for it and I am glad that I was able to express that appreciation to him. He was very much a "character" in the Blaisdon village of the 1950s. Pat's children made their way and did well in the world having required skills to ensure productive and purposeful lives. That's the measure of a father despite the drawbacks of an early life that Pat knew with the most minimal of early opportunities.

Pat Tobin rated himself worthier and higher than labourer status seeing himself rightly as a highly skilled stockman and agricultural craftsman.

In the words of James Bryant Conant: "*Each honest calling, each walk of life, has its own elite, its own aristocracy based upon excellence of performance.*", I remember Pat as defined by those true and noble sentiments.

Chapter 10 – Travelling In Style

In the years up to 1957, the farm workers were more than content to have two-wheeled transport to get about. Up and down the road and Drive between Stud Farm and The Salesian School - Blaisdon Hall; along the main thoroughfare to the Red Hart; on down through the village to Blaisdon Halt to catch a steam-train. Then onward and around the local villages: Westbury Upon Severn, Flaxley, Pope's Hill, Little London, Longhope and Huntley. Further afield to distant (10 miles) Gloucester City. Of course, I refer to the humble push-bike. Most of the incoming farm workers possessed a bicycle as the former owner gifted or sold it on as they left to join the armed forces. In my case, there was none available as Johnny Dunbar (Senior Dairy Stockman) had taken over departing leading tractor driver Gerry William's racy dropped handlebars Raleigh.

Even so, I was able to resort to the very convenient arrangement at the time: the slogan in Gloucester's top cycle shop read: "Hire-Purchase - It takes the Waiting out of the Wanting!" Very soon, after starting work as (Junior Pig-Man) in June 1955, and although Fr. William Boyd (Bursar) would have kindly loaned me the full price, I made a Down-Payment deposit of two pounds and signed the Agreement to pay the balance of 12 pounds off at two shillings a week. I was now the owner of a brand new Raleigh Roadster with dynamo driven front and rear lights; 5 speed Sturmey-Archer gearing; cable, not rod-operated brakes, and a spring-down stand. A particularly practical and new feature was the metal guard, which completely enclosed the chain. Father Dan had acted as my Guarantor and his self-presumed bonus was use of the bike, as and when.

Now, about this time Ronnie O'Connor, a Liverpool born, former Salesian School pupil returned to Blaisdon Hall after completing National Service in The British Army and was employed as a painter and decorator under the direction of Brother Thomas Palmer SDB. His room was in the former stables. Ronnie, who often looked and regularly expressed himself as: 'feeling like death warmed up!' soon declared that "...he would not be seen dead on a bike!" That included the mechanized transport of George Austen - Head Landscape Gardener - who zipped about on his whispering all aluminium (Italian) LE Velocette motorbike.

Obviously nicknamed "Scouser", I prefer to remember Ronnie as "Two Fags Ron", due to his habit of rolling two cigarettes at a time - one to puff on and another to perch on his right ear. When that second one was smoked, it was time to stop whatever he was doing to roll another pair and so on. He was afflicted with a tic, which caused his face to twitch involuntarily. Ronnie put this down to harsh childhood chastisements in a Cheshire children's home, which he dismissed as "over enthusiastic correction!"

Proud of his achievement in completing his trade Apprenticeship - no streaks or variation of tones in his painting nor could the seams be seen in his wall-papering - Ronnie indulged himself amply in the leisure pursuits of drinking, betting, Darts and Shove-Halfpenny. Such pleasures were not confined to The Red Hart but a wide range of Public Houses in the surrounding villages. All these pastimes combined fully with his passion for second-hand cars.

As Ronnie had spent his military service in a motorised Corps, he was de-mobbed with a most prized "Golden Goodbye" of that time: a full driving licence. He soon bought his first second-hand car, which was quickly replaced. This in turn went back whence it came, to the scrap yard in Gloucester, to be followed at short intervals on further trade-ins by a range of vehicles steadily improving in style and standard. There were exceptions: Roger Allen remembers accepting a lift from Ronnie at Hinder's Corner and having to keep his feet on the central drive shaft casing as there was no floor in the vehicle! The highpoint was Ronnie's purchase of a Lanchester, to which I will return later.

Down at Stud Farm, we soon became used to Ronnie seeking help for his latest breakdown. No problem if the car failed to start at Blaisdon Hall as it was downhill on The Drive all the way to The Lodge. If it hadn't started by then, there was no point in turning left for Stud Farm, as there was a steady upward climb from the Post Office to the next downhill run by Blaisdon Church leading to the sloping farm drive. Might as well roll on through The Lodge gates and glide downhill past The Rectory and come to a stop at The Red Hart. From there Ronnie - after a few pints of Frank and Elsie Hogg's best bitter - would telephone Stud Farm and eventually, after getting permission from Father Dan or Brother Joe Carter, I, or a farm chum, would take a tractor and tow him in for repairs.

These regular rescue forays and the subsequent - under the bonnet repairs experience in the tractor shed - led Laurence (Curly) Stanton, Alan Ferry, Roger Allen and me to pool some spare cash with which we bought an Austin 7. Laurence was principal shareholder as he held a full driving license, having done his army service in the REME (Royal Electrical Mechanical Engineering) where he had driven and maintained Centurion tanks. Under his guidance, we all learned to drive using the field paths and open spaces that the meadows afforded, once the silage had been cut and lifted.

One evening, we all spun into Gloucester where we went to the pictures. After the show, we got separated and I found our car, which was parked up next to The Bonne Marché - the city's Harrods well. Selfridges. As the doors were unlocked, a not unusual nor worrying oversight, I got in and settled in the back seat to wait for the others. Presently, what we would have called a "Cheltenham Type" wearing a trilby hat and smoothing his moustache walked towards our car and inserting a key opened the door and got in. I sat still. Then he took off his hat and as he turned to place it behind him, he saw me. "What the..! Who the devil are you?" he shouted in a posh voice. "I'm waiting for my mates" I said. "Get out immediately!" he ordered "I am calling a policeman!"

I realised, as I looked past the irate gent through the windscreen that I was in the wrong car for, two cars ahead in the line of parked cars, I could see my chums standing next to our Austin 7 and looking around. I had got into an identical vehicle. I jumped out mumbling apologies as the man started his car and drove off. If laughter was a fuel in the Austin 7 petrol tank it lasted long after the ten miles we needed to get back to Blaisdon and remembering the incident still tickles me to this day.

Ronnie's Lanchester - bought second hand - introduced us to the luxury end of 1950's motoring. This marque was out of the Rolls-Royce, Daimler and Bentley stable and when seen in its natural *mileau* was invariably driven by a chauffeur. What a motor! Four lavishly lined doors; beautifully appointed wooden and leather interior; crafted tasselled rope hand grips and deep pile carpets. Four passengers fitted comfortably in the back seat, two drop-down hinged seats facing them while three passengers could occupy the front seat. All this and built like a tank. A loud throaty klaxon hooted with a press on its foot control.

One evening, returning from watching professional wrestling in Gloucester Baths, we were bowling along downhill and approaching Birdwood. Ronnie was at the controls and six passengers were on board. Suddenly there was an almighty bang and the car's rear tilted down and to the right. In the headlights, we saw a wheel running perfectly straight ahead, keeping perfectly in line with the white marking in the middle of the road, then disappear. "We're on fire!" shouted Roger Allan and looking out the rear window we could see sparks were flying up as the axle scraped along the road. The scraping noise was combined with an ear-splitting squeal. "Everyone shift over to the left side!" Ronnie shouted. Five of us complied. The sparks and squealing stopped as we careered on - now on three wheels!

Ahead, the King's Head drinkers piled out of the pub, as a tyred wheel from nowhere thumped into the side of the bar wall, bounced off and landed in a tree. Then, out of the darkness, the Lanchester loomed as Ronnie managed to bring it to a wobbling screeching stop. With the willing drinker's help, we eased the stricken vehicle off the road. Luckily, as everyone in the pub seemed to know Ronnie, the Last Rounds bell had sounded, so thirsty Ronnie and me set off to Huntley Police Station and he knocked up the Sergeant who lent him an oil lamp to position by the car until morning.

Next day, Brother Joe, having diagnosed a broken half shaft, towed the amazingly undamaged car to Stud Farm. It wasn't long before Ronnie had the Lanchester back on the road fully taxed and insured. For some considerable time after that, we kept to our Austin 7, a lucky number perhaps.

Chapter 11 – A Birth Revisited

The devotional song "*All in the April Evening*" reminds me of spring times in Blaisdon, Gloucestershire. In that season, sometime in the 1970s Jim Kenneally, Lawrence Stanton and I are walking near Huntley – a distant village - and sheep with their new-born lambs are dotted about the fields. Jim is on holiday and is staying in Lawrence's home. The words of the song also led me back to the early 1950s when Jim was staying under the usual ad hoc arrangements with us all in the farmhouse at Stud Farm, which was attached to the boy's school: *Blaisdon Hall*.

Hospitality hosts Father Daniel (Major Domo) Brothers Joe Carter, Chief Cook, and John Wrigley, Head egg/bottle washer. Lawrence "Curly" Stanton, principal supplier of popular music - Danssette Record Player

Fr. Dan Lucey & Bro. Joe Carter Harvesting oats, 1958

Owner, Alan Ferry, principal supplier of classical music - EKHO record player owner, John Dunbar, Rock 'n' Roll, having changed from dedicated appreciation of David Whitfield and Mario Lanza to Elvis Presley. Alongside Jim in the upstairs dormitory are "Brummie" Harold and "Galway" Jim, two wayfarers whom Fr. Dan has taken in and after a suitable period of basic nourishment and recuperation, some spiritual admonishment also, are part of the family. Tony Brady, boiler stoker and household fire attendant, is a dedicated Light Programme listener. Other residents include Bill Harte - former seminarian - now assistant cowman and religious maniac; Roger Allen on his regular weekend stopover having biked out from Gloucester where he lives. He is on a five year Apprenticeship in Engineering: a lover of any music with a good sound to it.

We have been looking at the flock of sheep and their lambs quartered in a field called Periwell; Lawrence, Jim and I are sitting on logs and conversation turns to the arrival of that day's morning papers. Jim comments on Fr. Dan's habit of tearing out 'photos of bathing beauties and any woman who is not fully dressed. Some of the worst "occasions of sin" according to Fr. Dan were to be found in the pages of The Daily Sketch and Daily Mirror. We recalled that morning's breakfast: it had been marked by Johnnie Dunbar losing his temper at the holes in his Daily Sketch, which caused him to chuck the porridge tureen out of the kitchen window landing it in a fresh cowpat. The milking herd of 40 cows was strip grazing outside there at the time and a couple of startled heifers charged the electric fence knocking it down. Fr. Dan was porridge maker. He also intercepted the daily papers left at Mrs. Goddard's, Blaisdon village postmistress, as he passed there on his way back to Stud Farm having heard boys' confessions at the school's daily morning Mass.

Though denied tabloid titillation Johnnie at least had a real girl of his own. He was courting Iris who lived at The Red Hart, Blaisdon village pub. I contained tormented longings - carnal desires - according to Fr. Dan, for her best friend Margaret. A blonde and of the same age as me, our mutual shyness cut off all possibilities of progress. Still I could superimpose her ever present face in my mind on something else. More than once Johnnie had threatened to leave due to Fr. Dan's censorship. He eventually left to work in the coalmines of Wrexham, N. Wales after returning to Stud Farm from National Service in Cyprus. In those days, a farm owner held dictatorship - in Father Dan's case benign - over his workers through his power of claiming exemption of them from Armed Forces service.

Having been in the Army, Curly and Jim were men of the world and they added to my very limited, though developing curiosity, concerning women's anatomy by exchanging views of their experience of the Reeperbahn. I can't remember whether this place was in Cologne or Munich but it was in what Curly called a red-light district where soldiers went with women who were called prostitutes. I learned that it was not used exclusively for this purpose as many squaddies went there in groups to enjoy the atmosphere of the many drinking places with a louche ambiance of singing, lights and music.

Both Lawrence and Jim knew a few German phrases like: "*Ein Stein Bier bitte; Auf Wiedersehen; Sprechen Sie Deutsch?*" and "*Mein liebes Fräulein*". The "full service" from the women, was not always the main purpose of visiting the area because it afforded other forms of recreation such as women displaying themselves in various stages of enticing undress. I was awed by their experiences and felt strange stirrings, which seemed to be threats on my innocence and the bond I had of maintaining sexual purity with Fr. Dan. who was my confessor. As rams dozed and lambs frolicked nearby, I wondered out loud how you went about servicing a woman. My experience of sex was confined to what went on when the bull or boar were involved with cow and sow and I was a required onlooker. I told Jim, who was not a farmer, that farm animals only take the male of their species at certain times when they were ready while actively refusing it outside those periods.

At this point, the subject changed slightly as in a variation on a theme, I recalled an incident with Bro. John Wrigley in another season: Christmas 1953. It was the plucking of chicken's time. A group of us - about a dozen - boys from the Hall were down the farm one afternoon. We were sitting in a circle in Bro. John's Incubator Shed preparing freshly killed pullets for Gloucester Market. Bro. John was doing the neck wringing. We boys as we plucked began to speculate on the sex of the birds as feathers fell in heaps and revealed the plump smooth skins. Begley cheekily - soto voce – said "Bre' John, I've finished fucking this chicken - sorry I mean plucking". We all chuckled. Emboldened, John Loftus, one among us, held up his almost finished bird and called out: "I wonder where's the cock's cock?" We all stopped in a fit of laughing.

Bro. John, normally very mild natured, and seen by the boys as a great laughing chicken himself, was out of sight in a sort of alcove making tea. Hearing the question, he rushed out and, grabbing a dead hanging chicken by its legs, whacked at Loftus who, dodging, exposed me to a direct hit. As the bird was half wrapped round my neck I grabbed hold of it and a brief tug 'o war ensued which ended with Bro. John holding on to the chicken and me with its head shearing off in my hand. In a rage, Bro. John made it clear that everyone was in for the same treatment.

Like a flock of panic-stricken hens, we squeezed through the door and, all arms and legs entangled, landed in the mud outside. Bro. John carried on as we fled towards the farmhouse and dispersed among barns, sheds and under tractor implements and machinery. Eventually Bro. Joe rounded us up and after extracting our collective apology to Bro. John, we were conveyed by tractor and trailer up the back drive to the school for disgrace and punishment detention that evening. Further expiation was made when we were banned from education films the following Sunday evening.

Now, as we lounged in my room, I told Curly and Jim about my special pin-up picture from a magazine called Tit-Bits, which I kept, hidden and often stared at in private. On the front of my wardrobe, I had sticky taped round three edges, a 'photo cut out from the Daily Express which Fr. Dan particularly liked. The top edge was held in its centre by a drawing pin forming a pocket. This 'photo showed a lamb sitting on the middle of a ewe's back. It exemplified complete contentment. "Think about the Lamb of God when you are tempted by the Flesh" Fr. Dan advised. Concealed behind the photo was another one Johnnie Dunbar had given to me. He bypassed Fr. Dan by buying Tit-Bits weekly with *The Melody Maker* in Gloucester. By removing the safety pin, the picture within could be slipped out. What was revealed was a studio photograph of a beautiful woman: a temptress to any teenager, "A Jezebel!" as denounced by Fr. Dan.

Stretched full length on drapery wearing a one piece bathing costume was Sabrina. One hand supported her head, the other rested on her navel. She showed an unadorned neck with hair framing an inviting face. Bare-footed, her long slightly crossed naked legs melded to smooth thighs and led to the merest hint of her buttock's divide. Her jutting chest curved to a barely discernible cleavage. Sabrina looked out directly, her lips were slightly parted and her eyes reminded me of a figure in a painting I had seen in the National Gallery called The Virgin Of the Rocks, by Leonardo da Vinci.

Jim said that Sabrina was rapidly becoming the nation's pin up and would soon take over from Diana Dors. Curly laughed recalling that Fr. Dan was particularly sensitive to her picture in the papers and only last Sunday sternly admonished Vincent Faulkenbridge when he delivered the Sunday papers to the farm. The physical charms of the film starlet - as Miss. Dors was called - were amply displayed on the cover of The People and her life story was featured in The News of The World. In those days 1956-59, Vincent, in all weathers, delivered by bicycle all the Sunday papers widely in the surrounding area. He was very popular. He had to collect them off the London train at Grange Court Station - a five mile round journey.

Just then, Bill Harte knocked on my door and handed in the latest edition of The League of The Sacred Heart and The Pioneer. He asked for and got the loan of my bike as he was off to the Hall for "Solemn Benediction and Devotions." Jim asked me if I had ever seen a picture of a completely naked woman. I told him that I had. It was in the same art gallery mentioned earlier and in the presence of a priest. Two years ago, I had accompanied Fr. James Docherty who was the school Prefect of Religion on a weekend International Gathering of Sodalities that was held in the Salesian College Battersea. He and Bro. Alan Garman had chosen me to represent Blaisdon. Among the many and varied London sights that Fr. Docherty covered for my sake, was a visit to the National Portrait Gallery in Trafalgar Square.

We moved through the viewing rooms and it was evident that my priest guide was very knowledgeable about the art of painting and its many representations, religious and secular, sacred and profane; in particular, Salvador Dali and Pablo Picasso. We looked at Dali's Christ of St. John of The Cross in which the crucified Christ is seen from above overhanging the world. The meaning of Picasso's Guernica was explained to me. We then came to a large oil on canvas picture called La Grande Odalisque by Jean-Auguste Ingres 1814. This portrays a naked woman who is stretched out on her left side in a pose showing a back view. She is looking directly out at the viewer and holds in her right hand an elaborate whisk made of peacock's feathers whose shaft protrudes from her fingers and is pointed upward. I was told that the picture had been hacked with a knife by a maniac once and was completely restored.

Fr. Docherty asked me if I thought the artist represented a perfect display of female beauty. Being 13 years of age, I had no idea. He then showed me that the beauty I was looking at was somewhat contrived. Ingres had added an extra vertebra to the woman's spine in order to accentuate the long curvature of her body. Jim said that

Sabrina was "a *work of art*" and as far as naked woman were appreciated in that way it was not sinful. That was Fr. Docherty's point. Curly, very down to earth, said: "You know what they say about woman in the army Tony? - They are all the same in the dark". Jim added that a woman could be serviced anytime as long as she is willing. He suggested we go for a drive.

With Curly at the steering wheel, Jim and I in the back, we went for a spin in the Austin Seven that Curly, Roger Allen, Alan Ferry and I jointly owned. About a mile away at Hinder's Corner, we picked up Roger. He left his bike in Mr. Nelme's shed. I took over the wheel - in those days you could renew your provisional driving licence indefinitely. We never bothered with insurance. Then, all seats taken, we headed back to the farm. With Stanley Corner in sight, we spotted Ron "Scouse" O'Rourke, ex-Blaisdon boy but now resident Salesian School house painter, standing by his broken down Lanchester, which he had managed to steer off road into a gateway.

We decided to help him out by getting a tractor to tow him and he jumped on the running board. With such lively company aboard, I started to show off and as we tore round Stanley Corner, I lost control and went straight through the hedge. Ronnie leapt off just in time. Behind this leafy barrier were sheep who took off in collective panic as we came to an abrupt stop. The car and occupants being undamaged, we watched in helpless laughter as the sheep departed making farting noises as they fled.

The field was soggy but we managed to get the car back on the road and left Roger to drive Ronnie and Jim back to the farm and get the tractor out to recover the Lanchester. Lawrence and I re-assembled the hedge and set off after the sheep, which had strayed out of the safety of Periwell. Presently, we heard the tractor start up at Stud Farm and above the top of the roadside hedges, we saw the heads of our three chums as they roared towards Stanley. Lawrence found a gap down in an area known as The Gully and all the ewes and some confused lambs were soon reunited.

The local talking point about the sheep was that they were imported from County Roscommon, Southern Ireland. They arrived after harvest time. A contact of Fr. Dan's bought and shipped them over by rail wagon in several hundreds to be unloaded at Blaisdon Halt. After walking them up the village road to Home Farm, they were quarantined until the Vet inspected them. Then out to the stubble fields of barley, oats, beans & wheat. Rams were run with the flock and the lambs appeared in abundance in late spring. I remember some ewes birthing and rearing - with some human help - four lambs at a time. Fr. Dan engaged a shepherd who lived in a makeshift shelter, during lambing time, among woods near the field called Croft Barn.

Foxes abounded and *George Austin* was often on guard with his double-barrelled shotgun. He taught me to shoot and though I never downed a fox, I bagged the odd rabbit and squirrel. These mammals were seen as pests in the 1950s and George was paid a bounty by the Agricultural Dept., for the tail of every dead creature. I learned much about the flora and fauna of the Blaisdon estate from George. The sheep all safe, we were soon together round a blazing fire. As Fr. Dan read his breviary, we made toast and tea, and the April evening ended with the singing voice of Ruby Murray's Top Twenty chart hit *Softly, Softly Come to Me*. It was one of Fr. Dan's favourites.

My first daily job, before starting on the pigs, was to draw a clean bucket of drinking water from the pump and leave it in the farm-farmhouse larder. I also had to make sure that there was a ready supply of kindling and logs

Robert Upton from USA, a temporary worker at Stud Farm 1958-1960, letting one of the litters out for daily exercise

for the farmhouse fire. I was therefore a drawer of water and hewer of wood & according to Bro. Joe: "a labourer worthy of his hire". I was seventeen years old.

The day I first walked through the village of Blaisdon in 1952, I was twelve years old. An imposing dwelling called The Tanhouse was empty & dilapidated. It was bought some years later by a woman and completely renovated. *Mrs. Eglington* was a former Lady Mayoress of Gloucester City Council & a Justice of the Peace. One day Fr. Dan dropped off a couple of bags of spuds to her, which led to Bro. Joe delivering a trailer load of logs sometime after. She came out of the house wearing a fur coat, spoke very poshly, and miffed Bro. Joe when she indicated that he was supposed to stack them in an outhouse. He said: "*We only tip them off lady!*", which he did. "*This is the way we always do it madam.*" I said deferentially - wishing to support Bro. Joe.

Jim Meenagham with Ardencote Traveller prize pedigree Landrace boar. The Tractor House, Dog Loft and Farrowing Shed in the background, 1958

Mrs. Eglington said: "As all you do is just tip them I will have to tip a labourer to do the job properly." She directed the remark at me. This annoyed Bro. Joe even more as in situations like this one he liked to be on top if it came to a play on words. He tore out of the drive at full speed with the tractor, revving as loudly as possible & I almost swaying off the mudguard.

Anticipating the chance of making a few bob, I went back after my day's work was complete. It was about seven o'clock when I pulled the chain outside the front door, which rang a bell in the depths of the house. When Mrs. Eglington appeared, I said I had come to stack the logs - if she had not yet arranged for someone to do it - picking one up enthusiastically from the pile. "*That's most civil of you*" she beamed, adding that: "*it's more than can be said for that man Brother Joseph."* I did the job and reported back. When Mrs. Eglington had expressed herself completely satisfied - after ordering several adjustments to my neat stacking - she handed me a crisp brown 10-shilling note. A tidy sum at the time, as I was paid 3 pounds, 5 shillings & 6 pence per week as a pig stockman and general farm labourer at Stud Farm. Ten bob was very useful indeed. In July 1958, we were all shocked when Mrs. Eglington was killed outright in her car when it left the road near Birdwood, a village near Gloucester. Although she was not a catholic she had become a friend of Blaisdon Hall, & a full Solemn Requiem Mass was held at the Hall and her family came. She was buried in Blaisdon Church under the Anglican Rites. I have never forgotten the fur coated lady and the ten-shilling note.

As I had missed my supper at the Hall - in those days, the farm workers went to the Hall for lunch & supper in what was called the old boy's refectory - I called at the Red Hart. It was run by *Elsie & Frank Hogg* then. I mention Elsie first as she held the Licence from the brewery. As landlady, she was very welcoming to us lads on the farm even if we didn't drink. I was a Pioneer in the Irish Total Abstinence Association: Brother Alan had recruited me through The Sodality.

Bob Upton, holding piglets from a
Litter of 20. Sire Ardencote Traveller
August 1959

Daily, I said the Pioneer's Prayer, both in reparation for sins committed by drunkards and as a personal sacrifice promised to "abstain from spirituous drink" for the rest of my life. Elsie was also very encouraging about me seeing Margaret; she soon reduced the ten shillings by my purchases of crisps, chocolate and a mineral saying that there was a message for me from Brenda Davis. It appeared that a sow was farrowing and the birth was not going well.

Elsie let me out the back door and I made my way up stone steps set in the bank towards her orchard, which Brenda rented, together with a pig-stye.

The grass was high and the low plum trees were in full leaf. The hedge that bounded the orchard stirred with nestling birds, & butterflies followed its curve round from opposite the Rectory. The hedge straightened past the village school, situated on the other side of the road, and curved again at the Memorial (to the Blaisdon dead in the two Great Wars) facing The Lodge, to end at Smythe's bungalow bounding the Davis' family farm. Presently, I was close to a redbrick built stye and heard from within the sound of low grunting and the calming tones of a woman's voice. I called out that Elsie had sent Brenda and me replied suggesting she needed help. "She's birthed three so far, but she be in trouble. She b'ist quiet now. Just wait for a while."

I cast my mind back over three months to a day when Brenda had arranged to have her Gloucester Old Spot sow served by our newly bought-in Landrace boar. Fr. Dan had delegated the job & the necessary arrangements to me. First, we had confined Ardencote Victor, the senior boar, at a safe distance from sight and smell of the visitor and loosed what was a junior boar into the paddock close to the piggery. As I had already been trained for occasions such as this Fr. Dan's principal command was: "I'll see to Brenda, send her around to me and say an Act of Contrition before & afterwards. Good man yourself - Bejaysus!"

On what would be the most suitable day, I could see in the distance of Harvey's Field, Brenda & her Dad walking a pig towards Stud Farm. The animal seemed frisky and inclined to bolt and I thought that it might not be ready for its meeting with Ardencote Traveller - the name of our pedigree pig of a Scandinavian breed. My doubt about whether a successful conjugation would be achieved was strengthened when I saw the sow charge through a gap in Mrs. Goddard's hedge. The wind being in the right direction our boar was already foaming at the mouth, biting the iron fencing and its floppy ears standing erect to get a better view. Soon all was ready. The sow was now steady after her lively peregrination: her engorged, shiny vulva was fully presented & when I pressed my palm down firmly on a place just above her tail she held as if rooted to the ground. I knew she was ready. Brenda had already spotted Fr. Dan and, saying "This be man's work!", left the scene.

With Tom Davis's help, I steered the sow to pass alongside her now very excited & expectant mate and aligned their heads. Glottal noises, not guttural grunts or squeals, were exchanged through the separating bars and, within sight of the boar, we eased the sow into a dead end passage in one of the piggeries. By now, the boar's movements were bordering on the balletic as I opened the gate: it veered sideways across the last few yards towards the fully on sow.

When not engaged in the mating state, a boar's organ is not visible and remains protected and coiled within its body. Now, as it eagerly approached the waiting sow, its twirling tip emerged. Gradually a long pinkish coloured rotating shaft extended to its full length and, the still twisting & spinning tip, already squirting vital fluid made contact with the sow's slippery vulva.

By now, the boar was on its hind legs and mounted the sow's back clasping it firmly between its front legs. Being an inexperienced boar it was crucial that the whole mating progress with as little stress as possible. Its aim therefore was assisted. With a small smooth cane, and at a moment of maximum thrust, I supported the now fully extended tube into the desired place. The closest contact between both animals was now achieved as they adjusted their positions & the coupling was maintained for about ten minutes.

Many things could have gone wrong concerning the tenderfoot boar. It could become impatient with its mate, tire it or attack it. Continuous failed attempts to inseminate could cause loss of interest, ability and confidence in further mating, and bring about a complete lack of interest in breeding. An important factor, too, was that this was a paid for service, and full & assured value was expected by the customer.

Presently, the boar disengaged and regained all fours. Success being achieved it was not permitted another go - although it was more than willing - and with the aid of a protective board kept between it and myself, I steered its charging, snapping, reluctant bulk to its nearby bachelor quarters. During this progress, the boar's manner became calmer and its organ was retracted. Soon it was

68

secure in its pen on a new bed of sawdust, and freshly watered and rubbed down with straw. The sow was escorted back to the village.

Author 1957

My reverie was interrupted by Brenda calling me into the stye. I crept in and crouched beside her. There was good light and I soon diagnosed the problem.

Three piglets had been born and were suckling. About half an hour had elapsed since the last arrival, yet the sow was still in labour. "Give me your hand", I said to Brenda. I measured it against my own. She had the hands of a man, so used were they in manual work. Mine, those of a teenager, were almost feminine compared to hers. "She needs a helping hand", I said. "You bist best" she replied. Gently, I inserted my hand into the sow's birth canal. She made to get up but Brenda calmed her. Wrist deep, I felt a piglet. It was stuck sideways; it had a faint heartbeat. I eased it out and passed it over. It seemed dead.

"Unbutton my shirt!" Brenda called out urgently. "I can't do that", I said, as she freed the piglet from its birth sac. As she held it firmly between her two hands, I fumbled with the buttons with my sweaty & slippery fingers. Two white mounds separated by a gap fell forward & Brenda then placed the piglet between them while blowing gently into the piglet's mouth. I dropped to my knees as the sow groaned deeply, then in quick succession - like a string of white sheathed sausages - seven piglets were born. I placed them quickly at the swollen teats, to which they were soon attached and sucking eagerly. Equally soon the afterbirth was evacuated naturally. By this time, Brenda had succeeded in reviving the piglet and placed it in line with the others.

Jonnie Dunbar – Author - Jim Meenagham 1957 *Author with piglets*

An hour passed, and I left Brenda with a litter of eleven silken "bonhams" as Fr. Dan, who came from Kerry in Ireland, called them. I agreed to come back the following day and cut the piglets' teeth. Sow and piglets made good progress with Brenda's expert care and two weeks later on a sunny day, I watched the sow parade them in the orchard.

Being a first cross and, as sometimes happily happens, the best features of both breeds were in evidence. Most displayed at least one black spot: one actually had two black ringed eyes while the characteristic Landrace floppy ears tendency was evident. All, but two, made it eventually to market. Two females were retained and, when ready as gilts, were brought to Stud Farm for the attention of Ardencote Victor.

In due course two further 10-shilling notes came my way. I had to wait a while. The Davis' farming efforts were of a subsistence nature compared to our hundreds-of-acres effort. In an amazing change of fortune, Brenda, who had once been jilted by a Blaisdon old boy, Poulton, married a wealthy businessman called Watkins. He bought Flaxley Abbey, when the Crawley-Boevey family could no longer maintain it. That would have been sometime in the late 1960s.

As Fr. Dan was my confessor at the time, I made a full confession of the above incident in the stye. "Father forgive me for I have sinned." The gravity of sin was by degree: sight, sound, hearing, smell & touch. I accused myself of failure in all of these aspects of a sinful occasion. "My child, it was not an occasion of sin, as you had not deliberately placed yourself in the situation. You were there by accident not intention. However, you should not have gone there without seeking my advice. You can sin by omission. For your penance say The Salve Regina." Through the grille that was placed between two kneelers - prie dieux - that formed the farmhouse chapel confessional, Fr. Dan's face was obscured. "Don't forget. In future, if Brenda needs help with a farrowing pig, - Bejaysus! - you are to leave the matter to me. Go now and sin no more."

Chapter 12 – Unsafe In The Arms Of Bertie

From time to time, Father Dan would send me to help a neighbouring farmer: to catch or restrain one of their animals say. Not that I had to do much running after Bertie Buckett's stock. He kept five milking cows on his smallholding, which was in sight of Stud Farm and about five hundred yards distance. It comprised a concrete built byre with five standings close to the road called Hinder's Lane and was set in three small meadows surrounding a brick built house – formerly the Game-Keeper's Cottage - where he lived with the owner, his widowed mother. Mrs. Buckett also owned a plum orchard, which ran along the road opposite Stud Farm and had the grazing of an apple orchard on land by Blaisdon Mill and bounded by Veltehouse Lane directly opposite the bottom of Blaisdon Hall Park.

Bertie never drove his cows there; they followed him, as wearing his long brown overall coat, he went ahead on his bicycle. Each morning, in contrast to Stud Farm's twenty, two ten gallon churns were left at their farm gate for collection by the Milk Marketing Board lorry. Bertie hand-milked his cows: all were complete pets who followed him about and responded to his soft-spoken endearments. He had hand reared them all and called them by name: Blossom, Bonny, Blondie, Blackie and Buttercup. The last named should have been called "Buttockup" because of its habit of walking behind you and gently nuzzling your posterior then lifting you off your feet with its lowered head.

Mrs. Buckett was of petite build, rather grand in manner and was not given to small talk other than enquiring after Father Dan and Brothers Alan, John & Joe. Weather permitting, she drove her pony and trap to Sunday worship in Blaisdon Parish Church which was a distance of less than a quarter of a mile and situated on the hill that overlooked Stud Farm. The pony - called Crimson - was moody.

Not being a keen churchgoer, Crimson played up and a breathless Bertie would call over while I was feeding the pigs on a Sunday morning to get my assistance to trap her in a corner of a field and get her bridle on. The matter would be very urgent as Morning Service was at 8.00 am and Mrs. Buckett must not be late. Several of these frantic episodes led to Father Dan suggesting that Bertie stable Crimson on the Saturday evening: Bertie complied and the problem was solved.

Bertie was devoted to his mother. It was "Mother this," "Mother that," "Mother says," "Mother has decided..."and so on. He was an only son. His manner was very effeminate and he spoke with a soft girlish voice. In the 1950's, this was enough to attract the label of "Nancy Boy" and make it difficult for a single man, especially in a small village, to make friends with either sex. Bertie had several times, when I had been helping him, proposed that we be friends. I told him that the kind of friend I was really after was the likes of Doris B. (18) who lived just up the road at Stanley Corner or Margaret H. (17) from Blaisdon village.

Bertie was a lot older than my seventeen years and I told him that as I had no relatives I would look upon him as my one and only uncle. As he was inclined to be keen to touch me and comment on my physique when we were alone, I pointed out gently that such approaches were unwelcome. He told me that when I had helped him he just wanted to put his arms around me as a way of expressing thanks: "Mother says that the boys at the Hall have never had loving parents." I said that the Priests and Brothers made up for that and besides at Stud Farm we did things differently as Father Dan discouraged any behaviour, which he saw as "best reserved for the theatre."

In manners of "camp" theatrical behaviour, of the Noel Coward and Oscar Wilde parody, there was no better aspirant actor than *Vincent Faulkenbridge* - Head Gardener. He had succeeded a James Callaghan who, in 1953, was mistakenly arrested in Gloucester: a constable suspected that he was *John Reginald Halliday Christie*, the infamous Notting Hill, 10 Rillington Place murderer who was briefly on the run. Vincent was in charge of the Blaisdon Hall market garden and as principal horticulturist mainly responsible for about fifteen productive acres situated down the back drive. He was a keen amateur beekeeper and possibly the most popular man in the village. Not least for his charming manner but for his Sunday activities when he delivered the – as Father Dan called them - "scandal" newspapers to most houses in the village.

Like me, Vincent had been in St. Joseph's Home, Enfield and after leaving Blaisdon Hall had as he put it "lived in the world". His experience had made him not so much broadminded but openminded. He could take and make a joke and invariably was in the best of spirits being the life and soul of the Old Boy's refectory where the farm and garden workers, resident kitchen porters, casual workers and visitors took their lunch and evening meals. I looked up to him a working colleague and friend. In his out of work hours Vincent dressed immaculately and I often dropped off and collected his dry cleaning items in Gloucester. On the rare occasion, I helped him out in the garden when a tractor was required and he had requested one: "I have consulted with The Reverend Father Daniel Lucey who is most obliging."

For a while, Bertie had been keen for me to go with him for a social evening. He particularly enjoyed Whist Drives and knowing that I could play at cards had suggested more than once to a reluctant me that I go along with him. I was even less keen when he said the venue was in The Mother's Institute at Little London, a hamlet situated between Longhope and Huntley. Some of the mothers of local girls were members of the Mother's Union and anyone accompanying Bertie would invite unhelpful conclusions. I was finding it increasingly difficult to invent excuses and was embarrassed by Bertie's insistent if well-meaning invitations. I had run out of reasons when Bertie told me that Vincent was joining him so why not me? This was a solution to a dilemma that had been created in me by Doris B's mother who had mentioned to me that Bertie was "odd": 'a queer more like!' said her husband, and that female company was best for the likes of the young men at Stud Farm. A threesome was ideal as I would not offend Bertie and cause speculation among gossips and more importantly the local girls about us being a couple.

A number of pleasant winter evenings ensued as we went to various venues together in Bertie's tiny two door Austin - the model with the winged A on the bonnet. There were mainly women at these social gatherings: Bertie and Vincent, in contrast to my awkward mumblings, were very amusing and adept at conversation and most of the laughter came from the tables in the room where they were placed. On one occasion, Vincent had to postpone: "a mix *up in my commitments and engagements."* he said as he arrived on his bike as we waiting for him. So, I went with Bertie to a Whist Drive in Westbury Upon Severn situated about five miles from Blaisdon. On the way there, Bertie said that he wanted to talk to me later about a particular worry. It was something about his waterworks.

The evening went off very well and unusually I was paired with Bertie and mainly due to his out of character concentration, we won the top prize. Bertie in his speech of acceptance of a glass bowl: *"Mother will be pleased etc.,"* added that this confirmed his view that he had held for a long time that we would make a great partnership. On the way back to Blaisdon I had to wait for him to raise the worry, mentioned earlier, as he made a detour to drop of an acquaintance at her farm near Grange Court and see to one of her cows, which was due to calve. As we drove along, Bertie broached the matter of concern and asked for my advice. I listened carefully as Bertie said that he was taking me into his confidence: *"I have not told Mother about this."* When he had finished I said that I could not possibly go along with what he was proposing and the best thing was for him to go and see Father. Dan.

"Bejassus! Tony! The man's an eejit altogether! You and Bertie are causing me a headache to be sure an all!" said Father Dan a couple of days later. "I was hoping that Bertie would be able to contain himself just for a little while longer. Now this will involve a lot of digging into and I will have to get *Cyril Baggott* involved. As for you and Bertie coming to some arrangement, I told him that I would not allow it. *"Do you understand?"* *"Yes Father"*, I said with some relief, adding, *"I thought it best that Bertie came to see you himself."* *"He has."* said Father Dan. *"In the meantime keep away from Bertie until I've seen Cyril. I'm off to Nottswood Hill now. This afternoon would you be after getting the tractor and trailer, and pick up a load of sawdust from Forest Products. This evening, Vincent needs help to move his beehives down to the bean field. Good man yourself!"*

Cyril Baggott lived on Nottswood Hill - a traditional squatting area since the Middle Ages - in a wooden shack that he had built himself. A metal chimney suggested a stove for heating it and beside its door, he had sunk a well, covered by a boxed-in winding gear. The dwelling was built against a slope so one side was propped and the space underneath was used for storage, drying and hanging game.

Cyril set snares and it was not unusual to see him about with a rabbit or pheasant hanging from his belt. He was skin and bone. His face was the colour of parchment and according to Bertie was "as soft as chamois leather." When I asked Bertie "how did he know that?" he said that he dressed Cyril's occasional cuts and bruises. Cyril's eyes were sunk in their sockets. He gave an appearance of being scared and saddened by frightful sights. It was said that his experience in the British army on the Western Front in the 1914-1918 Great War had permanently affected his ability to communicate.

The old soldier rarely spoke and, when he did, conversation was not encouraged from his side. Cyril kept very select and trusted company with the village *"cider men"* as we at Stud Farm called them: *Albert Pitthouse, Tom Walker, Ivor Jones* and *Pat Tobin*. Father Dan, without being patronising, helped Cyril by paying him for casual work to supplement his war pension. Cyril looked upon Father Dan as a benefactor although his main friend and supporter was *John Dowding* who lived on Nottswood Hill.

It was not unusual to see Cyril Baggot (unbidden) trimming back or re-laying the farm boundary hedges or engaged in ditching. This work prevented overhanging branches from hindering tractor drivers or snagging in the combine harvester machinery and assisted the flow of water off the fields. Sometimes, just the top of his head would be glimpsed out of a ditch that he was cleaning. He never worked about the farmyard though, preferring to work alone always. He was the village gravedigger. He possessed all the country skills. He would hand-milk the cows on the rare days that Bertie was laid up. Cyril had one exceptional skill and it was this that Father Dan was going to see him about, as it was now urgent to get to the bottom of Bertie's   problem.

"My Goodness! There's enough sawdust in your hair for me to get the bee-smoke puffer going.", said Vincent smoothing with one hand his own well-coiffed locks which were waved from the back of his head sideways. It did not take long for us to move the hives and smoke-drowsed bees to the newly flowering bean field and soon we were in his room upstairs alongside the sometime Blaisdon Hall coach house and savouring Vincent's precious remainder of last year's prize-winning honey harvest. "I heard about you and Bertie, and Father Daniel is not pleased. While telling me off about the filth in

the Sunday papers and the corrupting effect on the villagers he said that at least Bertie doesn't get the News of The World. He must have asked him as I certainly didn't tell him: I have my confidences you know!"

"I recently started to get The Sunday Times," I said to Vincent. "Good for you" he replied, adding that he got extra money for delivering it as it as it was a heavier paper than all the others. "You learn about life by living it but reading fills in the gaps like music does. As I always say in the words of the divine singer Kathleen Ferrier: "What is Life? – If thou art dead!"

"I know the story of Orpheus in the Underworld, Vincent" I said "and often think that if I knew nothing about Christianity I would read Greek and Roman mythology all the time but Fr. Dan says it is pagan and discourages my interest in it altogether. His favourite book currently is *Miser of Souls* and is about the life of the Curé d'Ars, a seventeen century French country priest." "Mythology is all about living life through the senses. I'm not surprised by Fr. Dan's opinion: all those naked men and women cavorting in the woods and fields." said Vincent. "At least the Goddess Diana wears a skirt, however skimpy…" I said. Can I change the subject and talk about you and Bertie's problem?" said Vincent.

"The problem for both Father Dan and Bertie is that the system for providing water to the Hall for more than half a century needs to be replaced. Bertie just happens to be connected to the pipe that runs up his sloping field and leaks are particularly difficult for him, as he needs good pressure to keep his byre well hosed and dairy equipment clean for regular Milk Marketing Board inspections. Bertie told me that the latest leak is muddying round the entrance to the byre but Father Dan reckons the leak is further away. When Bertie suggested that he and you dig independently of Father Dan's supervision, he failed to realise that you could be wasting your time and with all that spadework find an intact pipe. Father Dan knows that the pipe is in nine foot lengths and that someone digging has to locate a pipe connection as the work will involve an, at least, twelve foot long trench. You could be at it for weeks. This is why he is annoyed with you and Bertie. There's more to this than meets the eye! Hence the need for Cyril Baggott and some good weather!"

A couple of days later, through a gap in the wall of the pig meal shed, I saw Cyril sitting on the chopping log in Stud Farm woodshed. He was drinking tea from his white enamel billycan that Father Dan had filled in the farmhouse kitchen and brought out to him. Cyril would not go in the house but sat surrounded by the numerous cats while tossing morsels from a sandwich he was eating. Between his feet, I could see the hessian sack that he always carried with him. I was curious as something inside it gave it shape and propped it up and, as the cats showed no interest, I guessed it enclosed neither rabbit nor pheasant. Presently, Father Dan returned and gulping tea from a saucer shooed the cats in all directions then, spotting me peeping, shouted that I follow him and Cyril to Bertie Buckett's.

Together in a heat haze, we walked in silence past the pigsties. Father Dan was carrying a spade and bundle of short pointed batons. We passed the Pig Field and as we cut through the Gully Gap, the herd of sows, lying in the shade of overhanging trees, grunting contentedly, raised their ears and seeing us, jumped up and fled harrumphing in a cloud of dust. Soon we were at Bertie's gate. From there, as Cyril walked up past the byre and stood by the hedge, Father Dan took a line of sight bearing with the Pump House, which was visible at about five-hundred yards distance, and turning right about pointed in the direction of Bertie's byre. I had no inkling of the drama that was about to unfold. "The pump's running Cyril, to keep the bally pipe pressure high!" shouted Father Dan. "Aye! An' I b'ist ready!" called Cyril. He bent down and opened his sack.

Cyril removed what appeared to be a large twig and placed it in the hedge while he tidied his sack out of the way. Then he took the twig out of the hedge and held it with both hands. I could see that it was Y shaped and the forked sides were slightly bent to form grip ends. Cyril held these with his fingers and upright thumbs turned slightly turned towards his body so that the twig was pointed away from him and it began to move up and down direction. As I watched, I became aware that Cyril was not actively controlling the twig himself but that it was rotating of its own accord.

Then, as if bidden by some mysterious force, Cyril began to be led by the twig and it pulled him forward as he resisted; he pulled it with both hands still pointing towards his body as he moved in the direction of the twig, which now began to point downwards to the ground before his feet. Cyril was now struggling to control the twig, as it seemed determined to connect with the earth: his body bent with it and his face was tense. Then the twig became motionless and pointed rigidly at the ground while Cyril became completely under its control. He stood with his eyes fixed on the point of the twig while it trembled ever so slightly in his long thin hands.

Father Dan exclaimed "Bejassus! Cyril Baggot you great man you've found the leak sure an all!" With that, he banged a baton into the ground with a spade at the very place where the twig remained pointing. This action broke the spell, as it were, and twig and Cyril set of in search of further reactions. These were soon indicated by the twig, and Cyril called that they all seemed to show a pattern that ran in line with the buried pipe. Each time the twig pointed fixedly to earth Father Dan banged in a baton and soon a line of them confirmed the run of the water pipe. "Good man yer'self Cyril! I seen many a dowser in Ireland go for hours in search of sources for a well and Bejassus! Sure an all never find a drop of water!" He walked back to the first "strike" and began to dig. Cyril stared at the ground and whispered: "the length and depth of two coffins bist needed." and replacing the twig in his sack headed off in the direction of Nottswood Hill and was soon lost to sight in the deep woodland.

Very soon, Father Dan had marked an outline of how the digging was to proceed and handing me the spade and with a "good man yourself" headed off to the pump house. Once the pump was stopped, there was less chance of water rapidly filling in and weakening the sides of the excavation. I knew he would not be back, if at all. This was typical of him, as he would always start a job then leave you to it. More often than not, he would sit himself down nearby and read his breviary pausing every now and then to check on the progress of whatever task he had set. By now, I had dug many a ditch with him and knew what was required of me. The main thing was to expose the pipe without causing any damage while at the same time forming a trench that would not need shuttering. I worked steadily for most of the afternoon and dug under and around the pipe to reveal a leaking joint, when I had dug what Cyril would have estimated the length and depth of two coffins.

During this time, Bertie had come over to acquaint himself with the situation and began to fuss about the inconvenience, the digging would cause to his cows. Though they were not in milk at the time, they still were housed overnight in the byre and he would be bring them in from his orchard towards the evening. He was in a huff because according to him "Father Lucey and I are not speaking and Mother is very upset etc... etc..." He nevertheless busied himself with bringing bits of wood and an old wooden gate to cover the hole.

Next day, the fine hot spell continued and while I was cleaning out the pigs, Father Dan told me that when I was finished I was to carry on with the digging. He said that the previous evening he had been up to Bertie's with Brother Charles O'Donnell, Blaisdon Hall plumber, who had decided a repair job was possible. I was to take a bucket as sea page had filled the hole. It was well after mid-morning in strong sun when after exposing the hole and baling out dozens of buckets of water I decided to strip to the waist. Father Dan did not approve if farm workers removed their vests but I reckoned on see-ing him approach so his distance would give me time to slip it back on.

It was a messy and slippery job in the clay conditions but with good progress and the dug earth thrown up and banked, I was eventually below field level and out of sight. I paused to rest and hearing a noise above I was aware of Bertie staring down at me. I had no idea how long he had been in the vicinity. "What I good miner you would make in the forest if you ever leave the farming." he said. "Stripped to the waist an experienced one can dig and shift up to a ton a day!" Behind Bertie, I could see the drooping head of Buttercup. "I've been down a coal mine in the Forest of Dean near Coleford." I said. "How was that then?" said Bertie. "It was an edu-cational trip for Blaisdon Hall schoolboys in my time there. I am coming up for a drink of water and a cooling sprinkle under your byre tap." Bertie bent over the trench and offered me his hand for a pull up. As he straightened and took my weight, Buttercup nuzzled Bertie's bottom and with a gentle push tumbled her master down on top of me. We grabbed hold of each other and wrestled to keep our foothold and balance as we slithered in the watery confined space. Buttercup looked on balefully.

As we were both wearing wellingtons, our feet kept sliding from under us and soon Bertie's feet got trapped below the pipe. He began to get agitated and shouted angrily up at Buttercup. The loud "stupid cow" startled her and she moved away helped by the bang of the baling bucket that I tossed up at her. "Silly bugger" cried Bertie directly into my ear, "We need that as the water's rising!" Bertie was still stuck and began to shout "Mother!" "Mother!..." From Stud Farm, I could hear the sound of a tractor running which would drown out any shouting in that direction. So, I shouted "Mother!" "Mother!" reprising Bertie: "Mrs. Bucket to you please if you don't mind" said Birtie, pursing his lips primly. "Alright Bertie then, Mrs Bucket! Mrs Bucket!...."

We continued to wriggle about in the squelching watery mud while Bertie's feet remained stuck. As nobody could see us if they passed along the road I said to Bertie that we could make a flag out of his long brown overall coat: so he let me unbutton it and I stripped off him. We both clung onto each other while with my free hand I put the coat on top of the spade and waved it about above ground. The only attention it attracted was Buttercup who was shooed away as soon as her head appeared above us.

The sun beat down and the water rose and was tipping into our wellingtons. We paused from shouting and after getting Bertie to take over the flag waving I squeezed myself down to a crouching position and manipulated his feet free and he was able then to stand erect on the pipe. Now, he had sight of his house and comforted himself by saying that "Mother must come soon as she will have made my tea and never likes me to be late..." Then, we heard the sound of a vehicle approaching along the road.

The engine cut and presently the faces of Albert Pitthouse, Tom Walker and Cyril Baggott peered down at us. The latter laughed as long and loud as I ever heard him. Then as he reached his two bony hands down, he said to Bertie "I've often seen the words 'safe in the arms of Jesus' on many a gravestone but..." then, looking at me, he continued. "I never thought I would see someone unsafe in the arms of Bertie!" Then the three rescuers pulled us out and after half dragging us to the byre threw refreshing buckets of water over us while Buttercup slobbered in the bucket to which was added a handful of crushed meal nuts.

Author 1955

Blaisdon School Song

Saint Michael stands
Stands at Heaven's gate
Saint Michael stands at Heaven's gate
And leans upon his sword
He sees a hundred hands
A hundred hands that toil
He sees a hundred hands that toil
At plough and spade and board
At plough and spade and board

(Sung to the tune of Sir Edward Elgar's Pomp and Circumstance, No. 4)

Chapter 13 – Putting Peggy Down

Stud Farm had long ceased by the 1950's, to be a place for the breeding, training and management of horses. Yet evocations of former times continually intruded into the everyday presence of the agricultural tractors. The chain harrows once dragged by horses were still in use. The once drawn by horses hay-rake was still in season attached to the tractor and its long rear projecting seat was a much prized place from which to observe the sweating workers turning the drying grass with their pitchforks. The pig meal-house, was my domain. There, the wooden pegs from which once hung the horse reins and bridles, still held oddments of the old equipage. The onetime horses stables had been converted to piggeries and the former horse looseboxes contained calves and the stock bulls.

It was on this farm that a colt was born in 1894. It was to become world famous as the *Shire Stallion,* known by the name *Blaisdon Conqueror*. This superb specimen of its breed was bred by *Peter Stubbs* the owner of Blaisdon Hall (1890-1906). In its prime, it stood at a height of 17 Hands and two inches. Its owner showed Blaisdon Conqueror extensively in the West of England and it was presented in London where it was a prize-winner at *The Islington Shire Horse Show* in the years 1899, 1902 & 1904. *Blaisdon Conqueror* died in October 1904 at Stud Farm after swallowing a button, which rotted inside its gut and caused death by slow poisoning. Such was the uniqueness of Blaisdon Conqueror. Its bones are preserved in *The British Science Museum*.

By the mid 1950's, the agricultural tractor had totally replaced the work of horses at Stud Farm and I would perhaps never had the chance of working with a horse, much less experience an especially historic moment in Blaisdon's history of horse management and welfare, but for the arrival of a *Welsh Cob* named *Peggy*. At that time, Stud Farm also had the extended management of the farm at Beckford, Worcestershire where the Salesian theologians studied in Beckford Hall; it was situated about 40 miles away. It was no longer stocked but cereals were cropped and transported to Blaisdon until Beckford was closed in about 1957 and the farm sold. All that remained was Peggy, a general-purpose farm animal that was brought to Blaisdon on a day in early July.

Father Dan had a few days earlier got me to take out a tractor and chain harrow the pig field. This was to spread out and disperse the droppings of the boar and twenty sows. On arrival, Peggy was turned out into the Pig Field and her care handed over to me. She was not pleased about her new situation and seeing the pig free grass and plum trees on the other side of the farm drive made two jumps, which cleared each fence and ensconced herself in the orchard. Hay, nuts and water were provided daily and she settled.

On a blazing August Bank Holiday Monday, Father Dan instructed me to take Peggy to Grange Court Railway Station and have her weighed and bring back the weight ticket. She was easily caught and bridled with blinkers and reined with a snaffle bit. With a thick hessian sack as saddle and no stirrups I was positioned on her back and after a few preliminary strolls round the farmyard I set off for our destination over two miles away. Apart from a short ride on a seaside donkey at Southend, Essex, this was my first proper riding experience. Fortunately for me, Peggy was used to being ridden and walked quietly with a steady pace.

We got as far as Blaisdon Church and as the road sloped down to the Post Office Peggy's paced quickened. As bad luck would have it, a group of Blaisdon Hall schoolboys came into sight and to shouts of *"Here come Hoppalong, Tom Mix, Gene Autry etc..."* Peggy stopped in expectation of patting I supposed. As the boys gathered round she suddenly put her head down having spotted tempting grass and I slid over her mane and landed in the dense white parsley but still holding onto the reins. I was quickly able to remount thanks to the bank and soon recovered my dignity.

It took over an hour to get to Grange Court. While the Station Master read and noted the details off the scale within the weighing shed, I steadied Peggy on the unfamiliar surface of the metal platform outside while obeying his instructions to keep my feet clear and maintain arm's length control. I returned without incident to Stud Farm and after losing Peggy into the orchard handed over a sealed envelope to Father Dan.

The following afternoon, a tipper lorry came slowly down the drive and halted close up to the straw barn at the top of the piggeries. The driver approached me and said "I b'ist here for the horse". I went to find Father Dan but met him approaching. He seemed irritated with me being on the scene and said curtly "That will be the knacker - fetch Peggy from the orchard - use the blinkers!" She came quietly and I halted her close up to the great wall of straw directly behind the lorry and within sight of a rusting erstwhile horse-drawn plough. Father Dan took over as the driver waited.

I turned away and in that moment I heard a loud bang and as I looked towards Peggy, I saw her collapse and fall against the wall of straw: the man stood back, holding in his hand, a squat pistol with a short spike protruding from its muzzle. The stricken horse quivered and her head lolled to one side then the other; it was straining back with staring eyes. I saw a hole in its forehead, dead centre in the white blaze, from which blood oozed. Then the man inserted a long thin wire into the hole and twisted it vigorously and the quivering spasms stopped and there was no further movement. Soon, the back of the lorry was dropped, a long chain was pulled out, placed round the lifeless animal's neck and attached to a fixed winch, which dragged it up the metal slope. Thus, the life of Stud Farm's last working horse was ended and, with it the role of the agricultural tractor replacing it, made permanent.

But there was one last impulse that I feel compelled to respond to. The bridle and blinkers, which for so long had hung emblematically on the pegs in the meal shed were still about Peggy's head. As the winch completed the slow winding up of its load, I gently cradled Peggy's head and eased it free of the leather and metal restraints then laid it tenderly on the metal lorry bed. From the meal-shed, I watched the horse hearse up the farm drive and, when out of sight, I replaced the equipment in what was its usual position and where it would prove in time to be its last resting place.

So it was that I happened to be the one - from the hundreds of farm boys - who witnessed the end of the last horse at Stud Farm. But, I want to leave the last words to a predecessor and poet who actually worked with horses there in the days before the agricultural tractors took over:

The Ploughing Team

"When dusk came creeping from the woods
and lent its chilling touch
to quiet the hedgerow's chatter
of chaffinch, robin and sparrow broods:
it was Time to halt the pulling pair.
Time to loosen the traces
Time to unhook the swing-trees
and leave the plough leaning there."

Mike O'Brien

Milton Keynes UK
Ingram Content Group UK Ltd.
UKHW051019060823
426262UK00005B/9

9 783732 396481